TOOTH
AND
NAIL

TOOTH
AND
NAIL

The Making of a Female Fight Doctor

LINDA D. DAHL

HANOVER
SQUARE
PRESS

**HANOVER
SQUARE
PRESS**

Recycling programs
for this product may
not exist in your area.

ISBN-13: 978-1-335-01747-5

Tooth and Nail

For questions and comments about the quality of this book, please contact us at CustomerService@Harlequin.com.

Library of Congress Cataloging-in-Publication Data has been applied for

HanoverSqPress.com
BookClubbish.com

Printed in U.S.A.

for Lucy

TOOTH
AND
NAIL

1

"If things get bad, go under the ring." Frank Costanza, the director of boxing, leaned down and whispered into my ear. He was a large man—over six feet, I guessed, because even with four-inch heels I only made it to his shoulders. He was at that ambiguous age when intra-abdominal fat filled the space above his love handles and hair disappeared from his scalp, only to be reincarnated on previously barren landscapes like ears and nostrils.

"What do you mean, *under* the ring?" I asked, but before he could answer an inspector beckoned him over to the other corner.

I was still relatively new to the world of boxing, compared to everyone else in the commission. The others had been around for years, lurking in audiences and following ringside doctors around to *earn* the right to work a fight. This was one of the first I had ever worked on my own. In truth, it was one of the few I had ever attended. But for some reason, after doing a few intake physicals and training fights, David John Jacobs, the chairman of the boxing commission, thought I was ready to work the corner.

I didn't feel ready, but I was used to that unready feeling. My whole surgical training was a lesson in faking it. But I wanted to prove myself at this fight. As the commission's only female fight doctor, I wanted everyone to see that I was just as good as the men. No, I wanted them to see I was better.

The Grand Ballroom of the Manhattan Center was brightly lit. Banners advertising *Dibella Entertainment* and *XXX Sports Drink* hung from the balcony. The ring was elevated by four-foot risers, and foldable chairs circled it like the petals of a flower. Four rows of ropes stretched around the edges, cat's cradle–style, creating the boundaries of the fight space. Like a bedskirt, a black drape hung in a ruffle from the edge of the platform. That must have been what Frank was talking about. I hadn't considered it a functional space before, but I noted it in my list of random details about boxing.

"Yo, Dahl! You're late!" It was Tom Marino. I could never remember his job title, but he was the one I went to with all my questions. As always, he dressed his lanky frame in a billowy, oversize suit.

"What? I thought I was early," I said, trying to hide my nerves.

"Nah, just busting your chops. Relax. You *are* early."

Tom alternated between my closest ally and the most irritating of kid brothers. He hated that he was the youngest of the herd of full-time commission employees almost as much as he hated that he couldn't grow a full beard. But that didn't stop him from trying.

I cupped his cheeks, fully aware of how much it bothered him. "You are such a baby face, Tom."

"Nah, I'm not, Dahl. I may look young, but I'm old. I'm wrinkled on the *in*side." He lifted his chin, stretching his neck over the collar. "I'll see you later. You're working the blue corner."

I didn't know whether to be flattered or offended. The blue corner was where they put the fighters who were expected to lose. For me, this meant climbing in and out of the ring all night, checking cuts and bloody noses between rounds. Or worse, watching helplessly from behind the ropes while my guy went down. The irony was that I wasn't actually helpless. New York is a rare state where the ringside doctor can stop the fight, but I'd never seen or heard of anyone actually doing it. In boxing, there was a lot more at stake than the boxer's life.

Giggles came from the opposite corner, where Frank was now surrounded by a huddle of ring girls in short satin robes. A brassy blonde was flirting with him. I could tell, by the way she leaned near his shoulder. Frank smiled and said something inaudible into her undoubtedly candy-scented neck. She looked barely over the legal drinking age. In Canada.

Feeling somewhat jealous and less than feminine, I was making tiny imitations of the blonde when Dr. Roy approached me.

"Dr. Dahl, I see you're moving up in the ranks."

I liked Dr. Roy. He was the most sincere of all the doctors so far. Practicing family medicine somewhere in Brooklyn (I couldn't ever remember exactly where), he had been working the fights since residency. Dark hair graying around his temples and moustache, his voice was broad and resonant with flecks of baritone in open consonants—the way actors playing doctors on television sounded. He telegraphed compassion.

"Where do you need me?" I asked, fumbling for my stethoscope. I realized I hadn't yet set down my coat or bag. Even though it was only 5:30 p.m., I had been working since 7:30 a.m., dissecting out an enlarged thyroid in the operating room. My feet were killing me. After residency, I insisted on wearing heels everywhere, even when scrubbed in for surgery. It was silly, a tiny nod to fashion after years of wearing surgical clogs. The unfortunate consequence of comfortable shoes was that my feet spread wide. Two years in, I was still working on fitting my toes into pointy, supposedly sexy shoes.

"Meet me in the back," Dr. Roy said. "We can finish up the prefight checks. Curtis is fighting, so it's gonna be quite the crowd." He wore the same tweed suit I'd seen him wear at every fight. And he always looked at me the same way, studying me the way he studied the boxers.

Even though he wasn't the main event, Curtis Stevens was the real reason everyone was there. A Brooklyn-born street fighter, he'd overcome a difficult childhood and was now a local favorite. Most fighters had one on-screen persona and another for offscreen, but with Curtis it was always the same. He was angry—an anger that was buried deep in his dark brown eyes. He was competing in the super middleweight class, so he had to keep his weight around 164 pounds. On his five-foot-seven-inch frame, that meant he was allowed some marbling to his muscles and excess water weight, so he didn't have to fight so lean.

When I walked into his room, he wasn't alone, which wasn't unusual. Even at the prefight physical the night before, he was surrounded by six men of varying ages, all shades of brown. One man, much older and dressed in a white suit and sunglasses, was praying loudly to the holy spirit. Curtis, with his light brown skin, short Afro, and stubbled, prominent jaw, was standing in one corner, rocking from one foot to the other.

"Can I take your blood pressure?" I asked.

Expressionless, he held out his arm and stopped rocking. I pumped up the cuff and listened for his pulse.

"Ninety over fifty. You have the pressure of a child." A few of the men turned and laughed. "I mean, you're in really good shape. Your pressure is really low," I said, but it didn't matter. I had made him look bad in front of his people, and I couldn't take it back.

Curtis glared at me but didn't speak.

"Okay, well, see you in the ring," I said, trying to escape as quickly as possible. The men were still laughing when I left the room.

★ ★ ★

By 9:00 p.m., the arena was filling with everyone from men in yarmulkes to Italian teamsters. I saw a sea of pink-faced Irishmen, too, which meant there was at least one Irish boxer—the Irish only watched their own. The rest of the crowd was a mix of all shades. One thing they had in common was that they were male. And already quite drunk.

I was seated at my corner on a folding chair in front of a table that abutted the ring. To my right were the stairs that led up to the ring. To my left was Frank. My eyes were level with the stage so I could have the most accurate view. I kept the necessary paperwork in front of me: a list of the fighters in order of their bouts, claims sheets for injuries in case one of them had to go to the hospital and consent forms for stitching them up if they got cut.

Three clangs of the bell sounded.

"Welcome, fight fans. This is the Friday Night Fights in Newwww Yorrrrk Citeeeeee!" The announcer ended the last word in a high-pitched crescendo. No matter how hard I searched I hadn't yet been able to spot him. He wasn't at the center of the ring—that only happened at the big fights, like in the main arena of Madison Square Garden. At these smaller fights, he sat somewhere inconspicuous, probably near the DJ.

"Tonight's fight is for the WBC Youth World Super Middleweight Title," he continued, as staccato horns and intricate drumbeats poured from a loudspeaker. A small section of the audience in the balcony stood and cheered vigorously, waving the yellow, blue and red flag of their country.

"In the blue corner, from Puerto Cabello, Venezuela, weighing in at 164 ½ pounds, with a record of 19-15-2, it's the Terminator, Marcos Primera!"

From my seat at the blue corner, I saw Marcos emerge and realized to my horror that I had checked in the wrong boxer. Because I hadn't introduced myself to him before the fight, he would have no idea who I was if something went down. Although I draped my stethoscope around my neck and wore horrible gray suits with my commission badge, no one ever assumed I was the doctor. The sparse population of women was limited to a few categories and, since I wasn't a girlfriend, official or stripper, no one really knew what to make of me.

Marcos wore white baggy shorts and a Venezuelan flag, slightly larger than the one his countrymen held up, draped over his shoulders like a cape. He was tall, around six feet, and lanky. His face was blank, but it was a different kind of blank than Curtis's. He was stone-faced and detached, hardened by years of pain. To him, this fight wasn't an event. It was just another page in that book of suffering he called *Life*.

He arrived at his corner and sat on the stool, allowing other members of his team to primp him. One removed his flag-cape, another dripped water into his mouth, while a third squatted and gave instructions to him in Spanish. Marcus sat there, his back to me, and waited.

"In the red corner, weighing in at 164 ½ pounds, from

Brownsville, New York, with an impressive record of 13-0-0, it's the Cerebral Assassin, Curtis Stevens!"

The DJ turned up the bass on a rap song, and the crowd went crazy, cheering and hooting. Curtis walked in with his posse, which had grown since the dressing room. He wore light blue sequined shorts and a matching short-sleeved jacket emblazoned with the word *Showtime*. When he arrived at the red corner, his manager removed the jacket, revealing a huge tattoo of a winged creature spread out across his chest. I was concentrating so hard on his blood pressure, I hadn't noticed it under the dim light of the dressing room. In the ring, it seemed ready to take flight.

The announcer continued. "The fight will be judged by Luis Rivera, Robert Gilson and Steve Epstein. The doctors attending the boxers are Jared Landau, Michael Stein and Linda Dahl. The referee…"

I felt simultaneously exhilarated and exposed when the announcer said my name. Frank smiled and nudged my shoulder, like a proud father. I self-consciously looked around, but no one in the crowd seemed to notice.

The bell clanged, and the fight began.

The two opponents slowly moved toward each other. They looked like marionettes, their bodies moving disparately but both from a central axis, as if guided by invisible strings. They attempted a few halfhearted jabs, not really connecting, mostly looking into each other's eyes. Marcos was a good five inches taller than Curtis, so he had to hunch down to even make eye contact.

Although nothing violent was happening, I felt my heart pounding. I remembered what Dr. Roy had said: always watch the legs because they tell you how the boxer is holding up. If their legs are shaky, no matter how good they look up top, they could go down at any minute. But it was too early in the fight for that. Their legs were doing very little except moving two steps forward, two steps back. It reminded me of a country dance I had learned in high school, except they weren't holding each other.

I jumped when the bell clanged. "That's it?" I asked Frank.

"That was round one! Relax. Marcos is here for the paycheck—he's not here to win."

"What do you mean, 'here for the paycheck'? How much do they get paid?" Marcos's corner men were pouring water over his head, some of which splattered on my left hand. I froze, trying to decide if it was disgusting enough to wipe away. I left it. I wanted to seem tougher than I really was.

"Oh, it varies. Some fights they get a lot, like the big fights. $10,000. $15,000. The pay-per-view fights are a lot more. But usually it's around $500. $500 for six weeks of training, only to have your head pounded in for the other guy's record. Crazy, huh?"

Crazy? It sounded more like desperate to me. I wanted to think of these men as warriors. The ring was one of the last places in the civilized world where men could channel this form of masculinity. They were lean and strong and powerful and fought in hand-to-hand combat. I had spent the last ten years surrounded by men with a different connection to their bodies: doctors who were so detached they could discuss bowel movements and open wounds while eating dinner. In my mind, fighters were supposed to want to win. I couldn't reconcile the notion of paid losers.

"What d'you think of that one?" Frank asked, turning my attention to the ring girl who was ascending the stairs. She held a card with a large number *2* on it.

From where I was sitting, I had a perfect view of her shoes: six-inch clear acrylic platforms. I tilted my head back just in time to meet her dimpled, thonged ass— fully exposed and freshly burned by a tanning bed. She spun around, revealing a bikini top that barely covered her oversize implants. I wondered how her tiny frame was managing to hold them up.

"She's your type," I said to Frank.

"Nah," he said, then, reconsidering, "I mean, yeah, but I only wanna borrow it. I wouldn't wanna own it."

The next four rounds were the same as the first. Curtis was more animated and lower to the ground, able to connect more jabs. Marcos just took it, barely fighting back. He seemed bored, like he was just biding his time until he could kick back and enjoy his $500 or whatever he was earning for the night's charade.

I was staring at a random fight fan with an eye patch, finally settling into boredom, when the crowd became excited. To everyone's surprise, Marcos suddenly came alive. He started pounding into Curtis, who looked just as shocked as everyone else. Barely mustering a defense, Curtis moved into a corner. It was all he could do to deflect the punches. It was as if Marcos, ten years his senior, had had enough of being a literal punching bag. My pulse raced in recognition. I knew that feeling.

Curtis cowered, but Marcos kept connecting the blows. The crowd went crazy, booing and hissing, screaming for Curtis to lay into him, hit back, defend himself.

And then it happened. Already much lower and from a crouched position, Curtis jabbed directly into what was right in front of him: Marcos's groin. Marcos screamed—a most horrifying scream—and fell to the ground.

The crowd went completely silent. Even the referee was stunned. We all just stared at Marcos as he wailed in agony.

"Why isn't anyone helping him?" I asked Frank, my eyes filling with tears.

"No one's allowed to. Even though it was a low blow, he has to get up on his own or the fight'll be called." He leaned forward with his elbows on the table and rested his furrowed forehead on his palms.

The referee announced, "Low blow. One point deducted for Curtis Stevens. Marcos Primera will have a five-minute recovery."

Marcos had the clear, singular pain of a direct hit to his inguinal canal. I imagined blood filling his abdomen, bowels leaking into a space underneath his skin but outside his belly. Pushing up with his forearms, he wailed again and slowly crawled across the ring, all bent fingers and flaccid legs. Everyone watched in silence. His pain was so visceral it reminded me of the pancreatic cancer patients on the general surgery ward at Montefiore Hospital. Their screaming usually peaked around 2:00 a.m., when the nurses went on break and forgot to hang the morphine.

When he got to my corner, he pulled himself up by the ropes to a standing position. The crowd started to bristle, and a low hum of discussion and confusion ensued.

Dr. Roy walked over to evaluate the situation.

"Can I check him?" I asked when he was close enough to hear me, suddenly remembering I was the corner doctor. A sob crawled up and lodged in my throat.

"Let's see. It's up to him," he said, walking over to the referee. He spoke something to him then beckoned me to the ring.

I went up the stairs and stood at the edge. "Can I check you?" I asked Marcus. Sweat dripped off his chest and face and onto my jacket. The cut under his left eye had swollen and filled with droplets of blood. I glanced down at his shorts, tenting over his groin, where his traumatic hernia was blossoming. I needed to take a look.

Marcos turned to the referee and said something in Spanish. The referee, an old white guy, answered him back in Spanish. I was embarrassed that, although I had spent five years in Bronx hospitals, I still hadn't learned the language. I could only manage a few medical phrases and the occasional term of endearment, neither of which would help me here. Finally, Marcos spoke one word I did know.

"Doctora?" Marcos asked the referee and then looked at me and shook his head.

"He doesn't want you to check him," the referee said.

"Why? He's injured! He could have a hematoma! Or, worse, his guts could be hanging out of his groin!" I said, raising my voice in disbelief.

The referee, recoiling at my graphic description, responded carefully. "He doesn't want you to check him because you would have to do it here. Ringside. And you're a woman."

I didn't know what to say. No one had ever rejected my help. Even in the hospital, when patients thought I was a nurse, I was more welcome *because* I was a woman.

Then the guilt crept in. What right did I have to be there, in this world of men? How dare I insert myself in the ring, in this setting, if I couldn't even do my job. I felt horribly ashamed; so ashamed, I relented and took my seat. At the loser's corner.

A few minutes passed, and Marcos was still standing. He had been silent since I had left the ring, but his eyes were different. They smoldered with dark rage. The bell clanged, signaling that his five minutes of mercy were over. It was time for round seven.

Curtis, unfazed by his show of cowardice, moved right into Marcos. Keeping his punches high, he pounded into Marcos's chest, back, shoulders. Marcos took the punches; he barely fought back. He needed all he had just to stay upright. Curtis easily won the round. The bell clanged, and the boxers took to their stools.

Frank's favorite ring girl tripped up the stairs again, this time with the help of a dreadlocked man. Her card now read 8. Visibly stoned, she turned too quickly when someone in the crowd catcalled, staggering against the ropes to keep from falling. She was the lucky one. At least she knew what her role was. I had no idea about mine, walking the line between male and female, leaning more to one side or the other depending on the situation. But mostly, I was lost in the fuzzy space in between. A manly woman. A wombed man. Deep down, I was really just a scared little girl.

The bell clanged.

The two fighters resumed their dance. I checked both sets of legs—they seemed to know where they were going. But, after the first minute, something changed. Marcos snapped. He moved right into Curtis, landing a sharp uppercut to his jaw. A stunned Curtis went limp and slumped to the floor.

"One, two, three…" The referee kept a slow count until he reached the number eight, and, seeing that Curtis had lifted himself up and regained some composure, stopped counting. "Fight," he said. But there was no fight left in Curtis.

Marcos, with all the rage that life and that low blow had lent him, poured into his opponent. His fists were a flurry of uppercuts, jabs, hooks and crosses. Curtis, still confounded by the head trauma, was defenseless. He had become a vessel of soft meat and bone. The crowd went wild, screaming, booing and cursing.

And, to my surprise, I felt a tiny smile creep across my lips. I rarely got to witness this kind of karmic retribution in real time, or in real life for that matter. And to be witness to that kind of physical atonement felt good in a way I had rarely known.

My reverie was interrupted by the ref, who threw himself between the fighters and waved his hands, signaling the end of the fight. The crowd rebelled, throwing cups of ice and pieces of garbage into the ring, pushing forward toward the ropes. The referee was quickly whisked away from the growing mob by two security guards.

The ring was now packed to compression with the teams of each of the fighters, the fighters themselves, officials and security guards. Someone had located Lou Dibella, the night's promoter, and had brought him to the ring. Dressed in baggy jeans, a Rolling Stones T-shirt and weathered suit jacket, he stood at the edge, clutching the ropes, where I had stood ten minutes earlier. Bald and hunched, he looked more like an overage rocker than an assertive multimillionaire.

"What's happening?" I asked Frank, confused by the delay. I looked up to the balcony at the Venezuelan delegation. They were huddled quietly, no longer waving their country's flag.

"They're figuring out the next bout before they announce the winner," Frank said.

"But why is it taking so long?" I asked, feeling a rush of anxiety.

"See these guys and how angry they are that their man Curtis lost?" He gestured toward three particularly heated men standing directly behind us. "If we announce now that he lost, there'll be a mob scene. Wait long enough, and they'll get bored."

I had never considered that as a strategy: delaying disappointment to quell a riot. It seemed to be working, though. The pause created a slow leak in the balloon of crowd rage.

Tom had somehow made his way over to us through the crowd. "Yo, Dahl, you okay?"

I wasn't okay. I was a failure on every level. I had failed my fighter because I couldn't examine him. I had failed the other doctors because I was too meek to work my corner. I had failed myself for enjoying Curtis's beating. A fight doctor has one primary purpose, and that is to protect the boxer. I had failed in that most of all. I felt more worthless than my first day as an intern.

After forty-five minutes of radio silence, Lou announced the rematch *before* the announcers claimed Marcos the winner by technical knockout. The ballroom emptied quickly after that. After a cursory check by a male doctor in the dressing room—a psychiatrist who probably hadn't examined a groin other than his own in thirty-five years—Marcos was whisked away in an ambulance.

Standing in the corner, the lone woman after the ballroom had emptied, I remembered what Frank had said at the beginning of the night: *If things get bad, go under the ring.*

Actually, that wasn't a new concept to me. It's what I had always done when I got scared. I tried to make myself invisible, thinking that if I got out of the way the bullets wouldn't land. I had made it through medical school and residency that way, but those paths were well lit by rules for right and wrong. When it came to standing up for myself and paving my own path, I was lost.

But Marcos had shown me something that night. In order to get what he really wanted, it wasn't enough to just step out from under the ring. He had to fight his way out of more than just that boxing match. Getting a bigger piece of the pie meant endangering his life and probably becoming sterile in the process. If I wanted more than what my life was giving me, it wouldn't be easy for me either. I would have to fight my way out, too.

2

I was first introduced to boxing by my husband, Adam, a few months into my general surgery internship in the Bronx. It was a time when weeks were measured in hours, and days were endless without the bookends of sleep. He must have been watching the matches for over a month before I noticed.

The day it finally registered, I was sitting on the couch, wearing hospital-infested scrubs, bloodstained and full of bacteria. Although I was used to a healthy dose of violence, it was too much to bear in my own living room. I thought back to the morning's gunshot wound victim—the source of said blood—and remembered how the two units I breathlessly delivered from the blood bank dripped out of his abdominal wounds and onto the floor, splattering my scrubs on the way down. Not the noble outcome the donor of that fluid likely had in mind.

"Did you see that? God! Look at the angle of his torso!" my husband said to the television. He was rapt. Hunched over a sketchbook, he busily scribbled lines and

smudged them into the shapes of the boxers. His fingernails were dirty with charcoal, which wasn't unusual.
That year, new to the Bronx and still trying to figure
things out, he had spent most days barely dressed and in
front of the television, working on sketches for paint-
ings that would never be completed. *Art is never finished,
only abandoned*, he would say, quoting Leonardo da Vinci.

I was confused. Why did Adam, the socialistic, self-
loathing artist enjoy watching boys punch each other?
Was it irony? He professed non-violence, ranting about
the military and gun-control laws ad nauseam. Did it
sublimate his feelings of being an outsider in a borough
whose residents were mostly Caribbean? Maybe he was
just tired of how his translucently pale skin incited angry
locals, and he needed an outlet.

New York had been his idea, even if it had been me
who had ultimately brought us here. He had wooed me
over pizza at Lombardi's in Soho when we'd visited the
city for my residency interview. At the time, New York
had seemed like somewhere we could possibly afford,
where we could live like bohemians in a downtown loft,
not struggling interns in resident housing. But just like
that artist's life, this boxing thing was a fantasy. I couldn't
even watch—let alone enjoy—it.

Too tired to get up, I stayed collapsed on the couch.
After a few minutes, I noticed something green and fuzzy
perched next to a half-eaten drumstick across the room.
It bore an uncanny resemblance to my cheese sandwich
from two nights ago. But instead of inciting nausea,

which was now reserved for disgusting sights of the visceral variety, it merely served as a reminder that I hadn't eaten since lunch.

Ignoring my hunger, I went to the bathroom to shower. I scrubbed with Ivory soap, but it was no match for what I had encountered at work. Earlier that day—or was it yesterday? I couldn't remember—I had been made to probe the incision of a new, post-op colostomy, while on rounds. Even sudsed up, I could still feel the moist warmth of bowel and feces between my fingers. After ten minutes of washing, I gave up trying to feel clean and got out of the shower to dress for bed. My filth had penetrated through to the inside.

"Good night, honey," I said, peeking into the living room. Adam was still staring at the screen. Although his preference for television over me was painful, I tried to conceal my jealousy. Since I was never around, it made sense that he had other love interests, but they were usually one-way relationships with inanimate things like video games, guitars, art supplies, motorcycles, computer equipment. I could already tell that boxing was different. His pleading for HBO finally made sense. And while I had agreed, I also recognized the real price. On my $30,000 a year salary, which supported not only the two of us but also his computer and painting supplies, that extra cable money meant I was eating dinner off unfinished patient trays instead of splurging on McDonald's during overnight-call shifts.

"Ooooh! Did you see those moves? He just beat the shit

outta that guy!" Adam squirmed in his chair, sketching the figures even more passionately. His hair, usually in a wild mess, was sculpted forward by two days of natural oils. He probably hadn't left the house or slept in just as long.

"I'm going to bed," I said and fell asleep to the sound of fists hitting flesh in the other room.

The next morning, I awoke in darkness without the alarm. Five o'clock. Adam didn't stir. Gazing at his naked, muscular body, I saw how easily I flowed into him. He was a necessary extension of me. The appendage that was free, creative, dark and allowed to express rage. Caressing his face, I kissed it gently so I wouldn't wake him.

I dressed and prepared for the three-mile run to Jacobi Hospital. For some, including Adam, running was exercise. A rush of adrenaline. For me, it was necessary transportation after my car was stolen.

Eight weeks earlier, driving over the George Washington Bridge, I knew it was only a matter of time before my car would be taken. Angry, tired faces stood on street corners in the North Bronx. Buildings were crammed together with sardine density. Dirt coated everything with gummy July heat. Parked on a side street, the Minnesota plates on my Acura Integra were as inviting as a tequila shot to a drunk. Someone easily drilled out the passenger-side key chamber, made a copy of the key and drove it away. When it was finally gone, I was partly relieved. Anticipation of the loss had been uncomfortable. I almost preferred the sober reality of the actual theft.

"Yes, I'm sure it's gone. I checked everywhere," I told the police officer on the phone, more vindicated than upset. "I just moved here two weeks ago."

"Welcome to New York," he chuckled, offering no help. "Now you can call yourself a real New Yorker."

The violation added to my growing sense of martyrdom. What was more, the insurance payout only covered the remainder of my car loan, so a four-wheeled replacement was impossible. The paucity of early-hour public transportation in the Bronx left only illegal cabs, whose fluid fare schedules and seedy drivers terrified me. I preferred my sneakers.

Scrubs tied around my waist, I stepped outside and breathed in the cool morning air. The stillness was as energizing as it was scary. Running at this hour, my senses obscured by headphones, was dangerous. I had to jog in the middle of the street to avoid the drug dealers in the park. Even the police officers were suspect. But the music seeping through the quiet darkness transported me.

In the arms of an angel. If only I could fly away.

In that otherworldly dawn, when morning shift workers replaced the night shift of gun-wielding teenagers, glimmered the promise of a new day. A promise that lasted exactly twenty-eight minutes—the time it took me to reach the hospital entrance.

Since there was no shower in the call room at Jacobi, I had come up with an alternative. I made my way to the bathroom on the cardiac telemetry floor, which was the most reasonable choice for two reasons: number one, cardiac patients and their tentative hearts never left their beds and, two, hardly anyone else knew there was a shower in there. Still out of breath, I snuck into a rusty stall, rinsed off and dressed in my scrubs, making it just in time to join my team for morning rounds.

"I told you to stop the heparin last night. How the hell am I gonna operate? She'll bleed to death!" Dr. Davis, in his usual dramatic mood, chided the overnight intern. Because he hadn't matched into General Surgery the first time around, Dr. Davis spent two extra years in internship. He was known as much for his comedic rants as he was for his temper—a temper he fed with healthy doses of oxtail, roti and coco bread from the Golden Krust Caribbean Bakery.

Dr. Haven, the intern, cowered, tears welling up in her large brown eyes. "I...I forgot. I mean, I wrote the order..." I secretly loved watching her suffer, but it wasn't her fault I hated her. I was jealous because she was luckier than me, as evidenced by her enormous three-carat engagement ring. Unlike me, she had been smart enough to procure a safety net. That ring was her insurance policy.

"You WROTE the order? What, you think that means something's gonna get DONE in this hospital? You. Are. A. Surgical. Intern. That means you do everybody else's work. Trust no one!" Dr. Davis's lecture turned into a bellow, spit flying, jowls wobbling. "When I say *stop the heparin*, that means you stop the IV yourself. Hell, stick it in your own vein if you have to! If all you do is write orders, you know what that makes you?" It didn't sound like a rhetorical question.

"Um..." she muttered, squeezing her brows together. Accustomed to flirting her way through tough spots, Dr. Haven was at a loss.

"That makes you a *medical resident*, not a surgeon!" His yelling caused the half-sleeping patient to stir. She was an elderly woman, who had been struck by a car the week before. Although those injuries were beginning to heal, Dr. Davis had managed to find some obstructed bowel, and he wasn't going to let her off the service until he got his hands on it. This was his last year of training, and he needed to cram in as much surgical experience as possible.

Dr. Davis finally noticed me. "Dr. Dahl, where the hell have you been? It's 6:02! Take the book. Thank God you're on call today. Clean up this mess!" That seemed to be my biggest asset, when it came to men. The attention I got from them was limited to patients screaming for their pain medication or senior residents wanting me to fix everyone else's mistakes.

I took the book from Dr. Haven. It was a faded green hardcover with the word *TRAUMA* written across it in large, uneven letters. The title was meant to identify the Trauma Service, but it was more symbolic of how it felt to work on it. Every morning, our team gathered for rounds to review overnight happenings, plan for the upcoming day and suffer Dr. Davis's tirade. As the on-call intern, I was single-handedly responsible for everything, especially things that were beyond human control. My primary goal was to get *it* done, no matter what *it* was, and, especially, if *it* was someone else's job. All of these *it*s were collectively referred to as *scut*. On this particular service, scut often included things like drawing blood, developing X-rays and emptying bedpans.

I turned to a new page in the book and drew a column of tiny black boxes, creating the list of the day's duties. The scut list.

Dr. Davis barked out orders as fast as I could write them. "Bed 2 needs a bowel prep. Get all the shit out of his colon. I want q.4.h coags on Bed 4. Do *not* kill his vein graft. Bed 3 is too lazy. She spiked a fever last night. Get her ass outta bed, or she'll get pneumonia." He rambled on as I completed a full two pages of new scut.

After the last patient had been seen, he held his hands together and looked directly into my eyes for his version of a prayer. "Do not kill anyone," he said, bowing his head and taking a moment of silence.

The team scattered according to rank. Dr. Davis led a group of junior residents to assist him in the operating room. The senior resident, Dr. Cohen, who had barely said a word during rounds, went to the call room to sleep. The remainder of us, three interns and two medical students, stared at each other in the hallway.

"GI rounds?" I asked, meaning it was time for breakfast. It was the only break I allowed myself each day.

★ ★ ★

The hospital cafeteria, unlike the McDonald's that was located in the hospital lobby, was a quarter mile away in a building called the Nurses' Residence. Although no one lived there anymore, the name had stuck. I imagined young women, living away from home for the first time, clad in white nurse's caps and tights, with dreams of serving the sick and wounded. The purity of this image made the place feel holy and full of hope. It also filled me with sadness. Although the inhabitants had long fled this dilapidated construction, they would have been disappointed to see the empty carcass it had become.

Nearing the cafeteria, the acrid bouquet of overboiled eggs and burned toast calmed me with its familiarity. I grabbed an orange tray and dragged myself through the food selections: cardboard pancakes, a wallpaper-paste type substance labeled *grits*, pastel-colored watermelon and burned tubes of meat. I settled on oatmeal, coffee and orange juice and approached the cash register. After the cashier had rung me up, I handed her my meal card and grabbed a creamer.

"Fifty cents," the cashier said, dropping her chin and raising her gaze. Her scowl was framed by a matrix of tiny black braids.

"But I gave you my meal card."

"Your card doesn't pay for that," she said, pointing a long acrylic fingernail at the creamer.

"You can't be serious. Fifty cents for *creamer*? It's

creamer!" Before I could unleash, a male voice behind me spoke.

"Here's fifty cents. Just let it go, Linda. This is probably the only place in her life she gets to be in control. Let her have it." It was Dr. Gross, the urology intern and the hottest, most delicious man in the hospital. I watched in awe as he dropped two coins on the register.

I was stunned. Everyone in the hospital lusted after him, including Dr. Elizabeth Carlisle, the most callous of the chief residents. Nearing forty and still without a prospective husband, she had once confessed her true feelings.

"I walked into the call room, and he was just there. Asleep. He looked like a little baby without his shirt on," she had cooed, her eyes glazing over into her younger self and a time when she was allowed to feel vulnerable and attracted, when men were still potential companions and not just the competition.

Even if Dr. Gross was feeling sorry for me, his attention made me so happy I forgot about the creamer. Men like that never paid attention to me. And he even knew my name! But before my internal teenager could fully relish in her visibility, my pager went off.

"Code blue. Code blue." It was the Emergency Room. The real torture of the day was about to begin.

When it comes to the trauma bay, rules of decorum do not apply. In fact, they only get in the way. Things like personal space and modesty, which our parents and the civilized world took pains to teach us, are hindrances that must be unlearned so everyone can do their job.

Today's trauma victim was a young man who had been stabbed repeatedly in the abdomen. I watched as the trauma team went to work stabilizing him. An older woman, probably close to my grandmother's age, was cutting off his clothes with huge trauma shears. A younger man was holding down the patient's right arm while another implanted an IV in his vein. A female nursing student awkwardly grabbed his manhood with one hand, struggling to insert a lubricated catheter into his urethra with the other. Looking around at the team's faces, I was stunned at how calm they seemed. The patient was naked, screaming obscenities and flailing wildly, but they were too busy sticking tubes in holes and creating new ones with needles to notice or care.

"You—you're the trauma intern?" An ER resident—or attending, I could never tell—accosted me. "He needs a CT scan. Stat. No other injuries so far. He's going on your service." That was code for *You will be stuck babysitting this guy in radiology all afternoon to make sure he doesn't tank. And, while you're sitting there, you can fill out a mountain of admission paperwork.*

Getting a CT scan sounded easier than it actually was. Just because the patient was in the ER, he wasn't guaranteed priority. Now that he was on my service, I would have to beg or otherwise coerce the radiology resident into letting him jump the line which, in this community hospital, could be anywhere from two hours to two days. I eyed a stretcher near the ER entrance and the orderly standing next to it. I recognized him from my other visits to the ER, although I'd never engaged him in conversation.

"Excuse me, can you bring me that stretcher?" I asked. He was in his midforties, brown skinned and with an accent unlike anything I'd heard before—more distinct for the parts of the English words he left out than what he left in.

"Ya see it. Don' ya got two legs?" he asked, not moving. Each phrase peaked in the middle of a crescendo and decrescendo.

"But you're the orderly. It's your job," I said, shocked he would talk to me that way when I was just asking for help.

"Oh, really? It's ma job? Wot, ya too good ta gi'it yo'self, *mami*?" he asked, incredulous.

"I'm not your mommy! I'm the doctor!" My voice rose in wounded pride. Did I look like I was old enough to have a child?

"Ohh, Doctah. Scuuuuse me! Ya tink ya betta dan me, wooman? Ya give me ordas?" He was raising his voice, growing increasingly offended at how I was addressing him.

I was confused. Wasn't it his job to get the stretcher? Why was asking for his help pissing him off? A few months in, I was seeing that, in the Bronx, besides the hospital rules, there was yet another set of rules in play.

The Bronx had a culture that was completely different than surgical residency or even the Midwest, where I grew up. From what I had gleaned so far, Bronx women were supposed to be more flirtatious and coy. When they played the game correctly, they were rewarded with things like gaudy clothes, acrylic fingernails and little else that pertained to me. In the Midwest, it was different. The sparse population and brutal climate made defined gender roles a luxury few could afford. Women had to work just as hard as men. If there was snow to be shoveled or a tire to change, you did it regardless of what was between your legs.

I looked into the orderly's eyes, realizing there was nothing I could say to bridge the gap of our perspectives. No matter what I thought was right, at that moment, to him, I was wrong. And this was his world, not mine. My pride started forming words in defense, but I knew they would only make things worse. I pushed the stretcher back to the trauma bay myself.

By the time I returned to the patient, everyone else had gone. Now I had to figure out how to move him to the stretcher.

"Hi, um, can you move over here onto this bed?" I asked, which was a weird thing to say because trauma patients were rarely conscious. Even though he was lean, I knew I wouldn't be able to pull him over alone without causing yet another injury.

"It hurts," he said, eyes closed.

"You were stabbed," I said.

"No. This thing in my dick. It hurts." I glanced at

the catheter. There were tinges of blood in the proxi-
mal part of the tube, but the bag it was attached to was
filled with yellow urine. Although it had a rough entry,
it was definitely in the right place.

"You'll get used to it. We have to keep it there to
measure your intake and output." I explained his plight
in the simplest medical terms I could muster. He just
looked ahead, ignoring me. "Can you move over to the
stretcher?"

"Jerome," he said.

"What?" I asked.

"My name's Jerome."

Hearing his name suddenly made him a real person,
which upset me. I didn't want to see a naked man with
puncture wounds like closed eyelids scattered across his
bloodied abdomen. I didn't want to smell his alcohol
breath or look into his dark, bloodshot eyes to see how
he was feeling. And I definitely didn't want to think
about the plastic tube inflicting pain inside his penis. I
only wanted to see him as my patient so I could do my
job, like the surgeon I was training to be.

"Okay, Jerome, it's time for your CT scan." I awkwardly covered him with a white sheet and watched as
he transferred himself to the stretcher, lifting the bag
attached to his catheter so it wouldn't tug. The catheter
was kept in place by a small inflated balloon inside his
bladder. Pulling it out would make his current discomfort feel like a love tap in comparison.

Waiting for the scan, we sat in silence for the entire three hours. I didn't want to know anything else about him.

After a long day of admissions, discharges, post-ops and bowel preps, I had to draw Jerome's next set of labs before evening rounds. Much like in the situation with the orderly, I couldn't depend on the phlebotomy team to do their job either. "You ready for another blood draw?" I asked.

When he saw me, Jerome said nothing and held up his arm. His veins, thick like cords, reminded me of the boxers on television. He shared the same body type: lean and muscular. I easily entered the vein in his antecubitis—the inside of his elbow—with a butterfly needle and watched as the maroon liquid filled the glass tube.

"You nice," he said, drawing his tongue across his lower lip.

"I'm just doing my job. I have to draw your blood every four hours to make sure you're not bleeding internally. Even though you were stabbed, it's really hard to actually pierce the bowels because they kind of slide out of the way when the knife goes in. You're probably going to be fine. Your labs are good so far. I just have to keep checking your blood to be sure there's not some slow leak somewhere…" I was rambling, uncomfortable with the look he was giving me, somewhere between hunger and lust.

He stared at me, not acknowledging anything I was

saying. A tiny smile grew on the edge of his lips. "No, you nice. You thick."

I couldn't be sure, but I thought he had just complimented me for being fat. "Are you talking about my body?" I asked, certain I should have pretended not to hear him. He was attracted to the very part of me that I hated the most.

But something in me appreciated the attention anyway. Growing up, I had been so unpopular with boys that if one became the object of my desire he was harshly ridiculed. This hadn't changed in college, where the only men who had hung out with me had ultimately rejected me for other men. It wasn't until I met Adam that I finally found someone who wouldn't leave me. But that didn't necessarily mean he found me attractive. Not like Jerome. Far from lusting after my body, my husband was more fascinated by its unusual shape. He was an artist who appreciated discord.

"Yo' ass is fiiiine. The kind o' junk make a brotha wanna come *home*, ya know what I mean?" He closed his eyes and made a motion with his hips, causing the catheter to tug with each tiny movement.

Junk? Come home? Was he saying I was garbage? Raunchy or affectionate, I had no idea what his words meant. Rather than make a bigger fool of myself, I just left with his blood.

I came and went several more times through the night, each visit welcomed by Jerome's grunting and murmured approval. After the last draw, when all of my overnight duties were done, I passed out on a stretcher in an empty patient room for the forty-five minutes I had left until morning rounds.

"Where's Dr. Davis?" I asked, when my team arrived with Dr. Cohen. Regardless of the day, Dr. Cohen was usually hungover on morning rounds. Napoleonic in stature, his body reminded me of a superhero figurine with tiny, tight muscles. I simultaneously hated him and wanted him to like me, the way nerdy kids felt about bullies in school. His presence was a constant reminder of how eager I was to be cool and how unlikely I was ever going to be.

"It's Saturday, Dr. Dahl, which means I'm on call. Can we please proceed with rounds so I can go lie down?" He pursed his full lips and swayed a little, holding on to the nurses' station counter so he wouldn't fall.

"We had six admissions. Bed 3 is out of bed, passing gas. Her X-ray was clear, so no pneumonia. She's ready to go. Bed 4 is post-op day 1. His osteotomy put out 30 cc of green mucous, so—" My litany of disgusting facts was interrupted by a commotion down the hall. I turned to see Jerome, clad only in a towel, charging toward our group. The elderly security guard, asleep at the nurses' station, snorted, rousing slightly from the noise.

By the time Jerome reached us he was yelling, "I gotta get outta here! Where the fuck my clothes?" Shocked by his sudden personality change, I thought, like Dr. Cohen, that maybe the alcohol and drugs from the night before had worn off.

"Who are you?" Dr. Cohen asked Jerome as he approached, backing away slightly. As a senior resident, he was not accustomed to direct contact with patients.

"Who the fuck is you? Gimme my clothes!" Jerome was still yelling, stepping closer to Dr. Cohen, who was a good seven inches shorter than him.

I moved to the front of the group, thinking that if Jerome saw me he would calm down. After last night, I was practically his girlfriend. "Jerome," I said. "We are just here to help you. Relax."

"Relax? What the fuck wrong with you, white bitch? My name is Murda King, not no damn Jerome." He got very close to me. So close I could feel his warm breath on my cheeks.

I had spent most of my life being ridiculed for trying, and failing, to pass as white in the Midwest. The irony of finally being hailed as such when it was meant as an insult didn't escape me. Ultimately, the classification of color was more about power than ethnicity.

I tried again. "We are rounding now, Mr., um, Murda King. We will get to you when it's your turn. This is really disrespectful." I was starting to think he'd lost his mind. Maybe he was trying to show how tough he was around the other men.

"I tol' you, gimme my clothes, bitch!" He was not calming down. In fact, the more I spoke, the more agitated he became.

I looked into his eyes, the same eyes that were so rapt with me the night before, and searched for something, anything that made sense. "Jerome, I want you to get back to your bed right now. We will get to you shortly," I said sternly, hardly noticing that Dr. Cohen and the rest of the team had made their way over to the nurses' station, behind the security guard.

Jerome moved even closer to me, so close I could feel the warmth of his body against mine. Even barefoot, he was much taller, so he had to look down to see my face.

"I will hit you. I don't care if you is a woman."

I was terrified, but I refused to let him or anyone else see it. We stared each other down, neither of us willing to relent. Then I found what I was searching for. It was fear. He was afraid.

"Do you think you're gonna die?" I asked. "I told you, you'll be fine."

"How you know? I ain't seen no damn doctor all night! Just you—the damn nurse!" he said, nearly spitting the last word at me.

I was speechless. All the care and explanation I gave him about his medical condition, and it still hadn't occurred to him that *I* was the doctor. What an asshole! My fear morphed into indignant pride. I stopped caring about being right. Or being the doctor. Or getting hit. I let my pride finally have control of my mouth for the first time since I landed in this miserable place. "No. You won't hit me," I said. "Now get back to your room. We will be there shortly."

Our eyes locked for another ten seconds, neither of us backing down. Finally, he relented. As he walked slowly back to his room, the rest of the team audibly exhaled.

"You are *crazy*, Linda. Did they teach you that in South Dakota, or wherever the hell you're from?" Dr. Cohen asked, more animated than I had ever seen him. I couldn't tell if he was concerned for my safety or just upset that all the excitement had made his headache worse.

I was too angry to answer, so he continued.

"You really are clueless, aren't you? He's worried the guys who tried to kill him are gonna find him here and finish the job. His street name is Murda King. You can't call him by his real name. It shows weakness. And he probably has a record, so even if his rival gang doesn't come and get him, the cops will. 'This is really disrespectful'— are you serious? You think the world works that way?" He was mocking me, and he was right. Everyone understood the dynamic except me. In the Bronx, I was the one who was clueless and disrespectful.

I decided to walk the three miles home, in no hurry to get back to Adam. I wandered down Arthur Avenue, past Italian shops, filled with aged cheese and salty meats, and cafés with wrinkled men drinking espresso from tiny cups. This place was so foreign to me, I may as well have been in another country. I had no idea how to behave and, when I tried to draw on what I knew, I ended up even more confused. I had come to New York to learn how to be a surgeon, but how useful was my training when I couldn't navigate the culture? With my background, so used to feeling out of place, I should have been good at figuring out how to act.

When my family had first moved to North Dakota, I had to learn about things like country music and tobacco chew. I grew to tolerate grotesque food substances, like ambrosia salad and tater tot casserole. By high school, I had learned to back-comb my hair into the same eighties lion's mane as all the other girls. But despite spending ten years in the frozen tundra, I had never managed to fit in.

When I moved to Minneapolis, I fared somewhat better. Without the constant reminder of my family's Middle Eastern culture, I adapted more easily by mimicking my classmates. I studied how they behaved in class and maneuvered my way into medical school despite my obvious eccentricities. By the time I had graduated, I thought I had it all figured out. But *it*, apparently, was only time- and place-dependent.

The Bronx was a different kind of complicated, and no matter how hard I tried, I kept getting it wrong. I couldn't understand the place or the people or the culture. Hell, I couldn't even understand my own husband anymore. I just wanted to learn medicine without the crazy social rules that shouldn't have mattered anyway. But I was stuck there for five years. And unless some miracle occurred, they were going to eat me alive.

3

The subsequent ten months were a blur. Images and smells blended together like a montage from a horror movie: patients with missing limbs, intubated and unconscious, handcuffed to beds for crimes they would no longer be able to commit. Federal marshals, lazily guarding them, more concerned about the answer to 2-Down on the daily crossword. Baby mamas and large extended families crowded into curtained hospital rooms, feeding their dying loved ones more fried chicken. The pervasive stench of urine filling hallways, diluted by the sharp coolness of peppermint-scented floor cleaner. It was one long nightmare punctuated by crumbs of sleep, not the residency I bragged about matching into.

The irony was that, after all the hard work it had taken to get there, I had little more to show for it than twenty extra pounds and a healthy dose of bitterness. I didn't know if it was the Bronx or that particular hospital, but my training program felt like war. Unlike the majority of my peers, I didn't come from a medical family, so I hadn't known what to expect. So far, I had learned that I was trapped in a military-like hierarchy with no way out until the bitter end. In medicine, if you don't complete the entire training process, you can't practice anything.

The lowest rung on the ladder was internship, where I currently stood. Come to think of it, it didn't seem like it was on the ladder at all: it felt like the ground beneath the ladder. That first year, things like sleep, food, time, coping skills and bodily hygiene were luxuries, not rights. As interns, we learned that our only redeeming value was to serve everyone who wasn't us, which included other doctors, janitors, nurses, social workers, patients, patients' families and the rest of humanity. As such, we spent most of our time doing non-doctor work, like drawing blood, filling out paperwork and figuring out how to get patients prepped for surgery and discharged as soon as possible. I had to make it through the year without killing anybody, and that included myself.

Rungs two and three were occupied by junior residents, who could safely maneuver from inside the General Surgery program. They were still controlled by those above them, but there were fewer people up there. And since they had stepped up the ladder, everyone beneath them was fair game for abuse. Especially the interns, who reminded them of their weak former selves and therefore deserved extra punishment. Once, I witnessed an intern blurt out the answer to an anatomy question faster than the junior resident, only to find himself emptying liquid stool out of colostomy bags for the rest of the rotation.

The fourth rung, and arguably the best, was occupied by the senior residents. With little responsibility, rare call nights and plenty of daytime rest, they had time to translate the three years of indignity they had been made to suffer into megalomania. They were easily identifiable by their unlaundered scrubs and lack of human decency. When addressing a senior, it was good practice to look down at the floor to avoid eye contact. Or, better yet, speak through a junior resident so you wouldn't offend them with the sound of your inexperienced voice. The only desire of the senior resident was to improve their surgical skills, which meant searching for patients who needed surgery but didn't yet know it. They mined the hospital wards like hogs hunting for truffles, discovering gifts like the cardiac patient whose hemorrhoids happened to be bleeding or the eighty-five-year-old immobile diabetic whose left toe looked a little pale.

Chief residents occupied the fifth rung. Delirious with power and responsibility, they unburdened themselves by barking out orders, screaming incoherently and throwing tantrums. Invariably, six months into the year, after performing hundreds of surgeries, the chiefs became confused. Delusional from hospital staff continually cowering in their presence, they believed they were at the top of the ladder. Until one day, when they happened to look up and catch a glimpse of the real bosses.

The top rung was populated by the general surgery attendings. These were the doctors who had completed their training and had made it out alive. They were untouchable and, as such, could be calm or bold, show mercy or abuse, be demanding or thankful. They could do whatever they damn well pleased.

"Oh look, it's the *doctora*. Hey, I need ya to get my stretcher." It was the orderly from the trauma night, mocking me. Since our first encounter, I had become as resigned to the orderly's goading as I had to be in my position as an intern. But, with him, the abuse was different. It wasn't about medicine or hierarchy. It was about the way I behaved as a woman. And unlike residency, his torment had no graduation date.

When I didn't respond, the orderly tried again. "You tink you so smart. But you don't like to be a woman. You even make yourself like a man."

He was right. Although I had never been girly, I had become a bossy, uncompromising bitch to survive. I no longer had the luxury of being a "normal" woman, whatever that meant. If I seemed too female to my surgical colleagues, I was considered weak. And the very traits that made my colleagues respect me made this orderly hate me. I was a woman gone man. Over the last ten months, I had rid myself of all notions of femininity, including emotions, vulnerability and long hair.

A few weeks prior, I had taken a short trip back to Minneapolis. I needed some perspective, a dose of the familiar, and I wanted to see my classmates from medical school. My last stop was the Aveda salon school, my favorite place for cheap haircuts.

"Cut it all off," I had said to the purple-haired student. She looked somewhere between 19 and 26. It was hard to tell through all her eyeliner.

"You mean, like, a pixie cut? That would be cute." Even her Midwestern version of female was too soft for what I had become. I needed to go back to the hood with something harsher.

"No, more like GI Jane. Maybe half an inch longer than that." I had watched the movie, in bits and parts, a dozen times since it had come out. At first it seemed like a desperate cry from Demi Moore for legitimacy as an actor. But, as my internship wore on, I understood her character more and more. In a world dominated by men, to get what they had, she had to turn against herself. Her femininity became the enemy.

I watched in the mirror as sections of my hair fell to the ground. The pain of its loss was replaced by an icy kind of strength.

When I returned to work, I was met with exactly the reaction I had hoped for. Amid the labels of *dyke* and *lesbo* were hints of fear from the men who used them.

I stared down at my ugly green scrubs and uglier plastic shoes, stained with bits of Jamaican spiced bun. What I had become disgusted me, stripped of parts that I treasured but were threatening here. The part who liked flowy dresses and twisted her hair into complicated French braids. The part who tilted her head to the side and glanced coyly at a man whose attention she sought. The part who reveled in baking cookies for friends and gossiped with other women in quilting groups. I had bought into the belief that a woman can do anything a man can do, only to find that it came at a cost. I had lost the parts that gave me joy.

I ignored the orderly and walked to the back section of the ER, where two residents were spraying down a patient with a hose. He looked to be in his midsixties, with a body the size and shape of the Elephant Man. His ankles, swollen larger than his knees, were covered in spongy, suppurating tissue. The skin on the rest of his body had collected huge keratin scales. Although he appeared naked, it was possible that some type of eroded underwear was still trying to keep him decent.

"What's happening?" I asked the EMT. He was standing against the wall, arms crossed, enjoying the spectacle.

"Retired guy. He's a drunk and, one day, he just decided he didn't wanna get up no more. So he just stayed there. In his living-room chair. For a year. Talk about a La-Z-Boy." He laughed to himself.

"For a *year*? How did he go to the bathroom?" After all my time on the general surgery service, my first thought now went straight to the bowels.

"He didn't *go* anywhere. He just did his business right there—in his chair. I guess the grandkids were complainin' about the smell or somethin', so his wife finally called us. He was screamin' at her when we got there, callin' her names, refusin' to leave. He said she was causin' a problem for nothin'. Can you imagine?" He shook his head, as if he were talking about silly teenagers having a spat, not the tragedy of what was in front of him.

Internship in the inner city had taught me a lot of things: that the festering feet of homeless men are a treatable condition; that just because a patient is passed out, face-first, in his own pool of urine, one cannot assume he is well hydrated; and that pit bulls make better weapons than pets. But this was something new. This was the farthest limit of the human condition. He was alive and dead at the same time, existing in his own rotting corpse.

"Welcome, Dr. Dahl. Just in time for your new admission," Dr. Haven said, twirling a strand of hair in her fingertips as she spoke. The shift-work schedule of her ER rotation, twelve hours on, twelve hours off, with no overnight call, seemed to be serving her well. She was back to her over-primped self, donning butterfly bobby pins and a sequined hoodie that read *Holla* in scripted letters. She was even wearing fuchsia lipstick. I both envied and hated her for being so *female*. I couldn't even remember the last time I wore mascara, wanting to avoid the inevitable black smudge after a forty-hour shift. The only accessory I allowed myself anymore was glasses.

"What's the diagnosis?" I asked, thinking I could somehow deflect this failure of the social-security system onto another service. I was already thinking that Internal Medicine made more sense. He was obviously having issues with fluid distribution.

"He has hypertension, fatty liver, type 2 diabetes and lymphedema. We are still waiting on his echocardiogram to rule out congestive heart failure. Oh, and he has maggots," she said.

"Excuse me?" I thought she was describing his apartment. "What does that have to do with his admission?"

"No, he has maggots, like, in his lower extremities, which is good and bad. On the one hand they're great because they eat away the dead flesh, so…less work for you. On the other hand, well, that's just obvious. Throw on some gloves so you can help smother them. In a few days, you guys are gonna have to start the revolving door to the OR for wound debridement. His backside, where he sat in the chair all that time, is eroded down to the bone."

Maggots were an unanticipated trump card on her part. There was no way I could deflect him off my service with that diagnosis. Defeated, I covered my scrubs with a yellow gown and tied a surgical mask to my face, preparing for what lay ahead. Even though smothering maggots disgusted me beyond anything I had ever known, I was determined to do it. I was just as tough as the men, wasn't I? I had made it this far without giving in or showing signs of weakness. If there were maggots to be killed, then I would handle those little fuckers like I had handled Murda King.

When I approached the barely conscious patient, a medical student was already in position, kneeling on the floor like he was praying to the huge rotting altar in front of him. With assertion, he scooped a handful of Vaseline out of a plastic jar and smeared it up and down on what used to be the man's calves. Trying to mimic his enthusiasm, I pulled on latex gloves and dropped to my knees. The smell easily penetrated my mask, kind of a sweet, decaying odor. I had to fight back a gag by breathing through my mouth, which made things worse because the smell turned into a taste—the taste of necrosis. I slowly rubbed the Vaseline into the moist flesh, trying to block the feeling of squirming maggots under my fingertips. The flesh was soft and almost weightless, like the warm dough I used to knead every Sunday morning growing up. The incongruous association created a pause in my movement, a pause just long enough to allow the weight of my fingers to sink through the fluffy tissue to the underlying bone.

The gag that was caught in my throat leapt forward. Panicked, I stood and frantically tried to rip off my gear, which now clung to me like a straitjacket. Partially successful, I ran down the hall, past the technician and orderly, who were laughing hysterically. When I reached the front door, I thrust it open and bent forward, hyperventilating to clear the rancid air out of my body.

It was in that moment that I realized I had lost. This place, this internship, these people had finally broken me. No matter how hard I tried to be tough, I wasn't. Underneath it all, I still had emotions and weaknesses and limits. I was still human. And no matter how short my hair, I was still female.

My breakdown awoke the critical voices of every teacher and admissions-committee member over the last twenty years. In their well-meaning ways, the message was always the same: being tough was the only option. Girls can do anything boys can. Not to mention my father, who spent years lecturing my sisters and me on the fatal flaws of weakness, which he blamed on our unfortunate gender. He wanted us to be strong, which in his eyes meant behaving like men, competing with men and being emotionally impenetrable. But now that my tough, manly act had betrayed me, I felt like a failure. I would have to come up with another way to survive, but I had no clue where to start.

Very quickly, boxing moved from my husband's fling to a full-on girlfriend: the annoying kind who stayed over all the time but didn't pay rent. And she was getting more and more demanding by the minute.

"Listen to this. You get the prefight weigh in, three lower-card bouts, celebrity interviews and the main event for only $50! Can you believe that?" Adam's excited words woke me from a deep sleep. Although he had managed to find some consulting work, his earnings weren't even enough to cover the cost of the additional equipment he needed to do the work. Despite his efforts, we were even more broke.

I turned over and covered my head with a pillow, hoping to suffocate my budding awareness. But he wouldn't stop talking.

"De La Hoya is an Olympic gold medalist. His first and only professional loss was to Felix Trinidad, but that was bullshit," he continued, spouting statistics and facts, as if building a case would somehow justify spending money we didn't have on something I didn't care about. I groaned under the pillow.

These types of discussions usually ended in one of two ways: a huge fight or my relenting. I wasn't up for either, so I closed my eyes tighter and stared into the backs of my eyelids.

"Baby, you will love this! He's the best-looking guy in boxing. They call him the Golden Boy. Did I mention he also recorded an album? He's a rock star." I could hear him prancing around the bedroom, manic.

Pretending to ignore him wasn't working, so I opened my eyes and tried another approach. "Adam, why do we need to pay for this fight? Can't you just watch it on HBO?"

"Noooo. This is pay-per-view. It's the only way to see it. It's like having a private ticket with ringside seats! Jose told me everyone is pooling together to watch it in his cousin's apartment."

"Who the hell is Jose?" I asked. I knew Adam didn't have any friends. I was worried he was starting to think the characters in his Grand Theft Auto video game were real.

"He works at the bodega. We have breakfast together every morning. Good guy. He's from Puerto Rico. Then there's Manuel, he works the night shift. I like the way he makes the coffee because when I say *regular* he knows not to make it too sweet." He was referring to the fact that, in the Bronx, *regular* coffee meant that it was so drowned in whole milk and sugar it tasted more like sweetened condensed milk.

I couldn't believe it. Even spending most of his time at the apartment, the only Midwesterner on Wayne Avenue, Adam had still managed to create a community here. He knew people's names and where they were from. He was even developing something in common with them. With all of my interactions at the hospital, the only connections I had managed to make were the bad kind.

The Bronx reminded me of how I had felt when my family had first moved to North Dakota. Even at age eight, I knew that my parents' choice to reside in that part of the country wasn't logical, not for us anyway. They chose that state for its wholesome values, assuming those values would somehow leak into our family by osmosis. But they were wrong. North Dakota was so homogenous there was no way for Middle Easterners to blend in. Everyone was blond and large and spoke with strange accents, pronouncing open *a*s like long *a*s so the word *flag* sounded more like something that happened to old paint than something you pledge your allegiance to. And since I couldn't adapt to their strange dialect, I was the laughingstock of the fourth grade for speaking what I thought was proper English. The disparity between *us* and *them* penetrated everything, especially food choices.

One night, a few months after moving there, my parents insisted I invite a classmate to dinner. I had no friends at my new school, so they thought dinner would help me get over my shyness. The truth was, I was quiet on purpose. The more visible I was, the more the other kids would be aware of my existence—which was too short, too dark and way too ethnic.

I resisted inviting anyone at first, using the excuse that American kids didn't eat the same foods we did. "Don't worry," my father said. "Your mother's a great cook. She will make American spaghetti."

Cautiously optimistic, I invited Wendy Helmsrud. I chose her because, unlike the other kids, she hadn't expressed open disdain for me. Yet. Perhaps it was because she was too tall for the fourth grade and therefore felt just as awkward. Or maybe she hated me, too, but simply wanted to enter the foreign people's house out of curiosity. Nonetheless, she seemed the least likely to tease me at recess if it all went south.

To my surprise, she agreed to the invitation.

As promised, the pasta was served with normal-tasting meat sauce, my mother mercifully having replaced the cinnamon my father usually demanded with oregano. To my shock, Wendy enjoyed the oversize portion of food and the mound of grated parmesan. She even asked for more Kool-Aid.

Feeling relieved and a little cocky, I asked to be excused, thinking I could boost my social status even higher by showing her my room. It was spacious, with a canopy bed and a closet I had converted to a dollhouse for my Barbie collection.

"Sure, just put your dishes in the sink," my father said,

moving over to the oven. "But before you go, show your friend what your mother made for me. It's a delicacy where we come from!" He opened the oven and pulled out a fully intact lamb skull, steam rising through the vacant eyeholes. Before I could stop him, he had grabbed a chisel and hammer and started pounding away at the cranium. We watched in horror as he lifted the skull, exposing the shrunken, cooked brains. With a fork, he gingerly teased out a piece of the white matter and took a bite.

The look of horror on Wendy's face remained with me until graduation. Needless to say, the experience remained with Wendy as well. It served a purpose, though, giving her something to talk about with classmates who otherwise would have teased her for being the weirdo. And I was wrong about recess.

"Fifty dollars is a lot, Adam. But let me think about it," I said, making my way to the bathroom. I stared at my reflection in the mirror, barely recognizing myself. My hair was matted into a curly nest. Dark circles rimmed my eyes. Fat bulged over the edges of my underwear, extra padding from the late night carbohydrate binges that would keep me awake when the caffeine stopped working. Looking down at my expanded belly, I remembered a trick a friend from medical school had once shown me: that if I squeezed the belly fat around my navel I could make it look like a bagel. When I squeezed it now, it looked more like a loaf of bread.

Maybe Adam was right about the fight. He was breaking me, but he was breaking me softly. What was another fifty dollars if it helped me learn how to fit in here? It was so complicated in the Bronx, maybe I just I needed to do more research. There were so many different types of people—in what area should I conform? In the Midwest there were only two ethnic groups: white and other. And since I didn't have blue eyes, blond hair and lanky limbs, my category was obvious. I was even nicknamed *darkie*, a sort of verbal confirmation of my place. And like my fellow *darkies*—the children of the Pakistani and Indian doctors, lulled into the freezing middle of nowhere by outrageous salaries, or the rare African-American daughter of a captain from the air force base—I learned that I needed to mimic the white people as closely as I could.

Maybe I had been going about it all wrong. In the Bronx, the diversity made fitting in less about ethnicity and more about common interests. Since I had nothing in common with the locals, I would have to find something to help me connect. Watching the fight could be my starting point, a shared experience. It seemed to be working for Adam. Maybe I could follow his lead.

As the day turned to evening, the neighborhood streets emptied. The Bronx felt almost ghostly, as invisible crowds gathered in cramped apartments and tiny restaurants. Everyone was glued to their televisions for the fight.

Adam celebrated his victory by ordering a pizza, Diet Coke and black-and-white cookies—my personal favorite. This meal was as close as he ever came to preparing dinner, so I accepted it as a gesture of his appreciation. Biting into the densely sweet chocolate icing, I felt the intoxicating rush of sugar enter my bloodstream. I was ready for the show.

I settled into the couch, kicking away half-read magazines with titles that belied Adam's breadth of interests: *Art Forum, the Economist, Utne Reader, Computer User, Wired, Macworld*. Our nineteen-inch television sat on metal scaffolding on the opposite side of the room. Above it, disheveled rows of CDs and DVDs were layered with torn paperbacks. To the right was a metallic tower of black, humming boxes, indicator lights flashing. Next to them stood three electric guitars in parallel, their cords woven together like a neuronal network, synapsing into the huge outlet strip that also received the television cord. The outlet strip reminded me of myself, exchanging so much energy simultaneously that one day it might spontaneously explode.

"Get ready to watch these two great fighters come into the ring. And they're fighting for De La Hoya's welterweight crown, and it is Mosley who will enter the ring first." The announcer spoke like we were already part of the team just by tuning in.

De La Hoya's opponent was "Sugar" Shane Mosley, the lesser known fighter. Shorter than his opponent, he had a longer reach, and weighed a few pounds more. They had comparable records, including things like average numbers of punches thrown and hits taken. The announcers listed so many statistics it felt like we were about to watch a dog show, not a boxing match. There was nothing about Mosley that stood out.

The cameras moved to him making his way toward the ring. He was smiling softly, led by his son and two young nephews. His face was shy, with long dimples and bright gray-blue eyes. He bounced to the blurry rap music in the background, casually high-fiving the people around him.

The announcer spoke. "Everyone has commented about how calmly and how well Mosley has taken this big occasion this week. As he put it, 'Why be afraid of what I want?'"

Why be afraid of what I want? That was a new perspective. Then again, what did I want anymore? Everything I wanted turned into disappointment once I got it. I had wanted to be a surgeon. I had wanted to be a wife. I had even thought I had wanted to be a New Yorker. I got all those wants, and look where it got me. In my case, maybe I needed to start being afraid of what I wanted or just stop wanting anything altogether.

"I've been watching him train. There is a small chance he could kick Oscar's ass," Adam said. That was hard to believe from the way he had described De La Hoya, but the possibility of the underdog taking the belt filled me with an almost aching delight. Mosley's confidence was so understated he didn't fit the persona of a prizefighter at all. Instead of trying to play up to what was expected, he followed the beat of his own drum. We had yet to see how that would translate in the ring.

The cameras cut to De La Hoya's dressing room, where he boxed the shadow that would be his opponent. His body reminded me of my college art-class figure model, all sculpted abs and powerful shoulders. Oscar's perfect nose looked like it hadn't sustained a single blow. He was surrounded by a posse of men in red satin jackets, carrying buckets and towels.

The announcer spoke again. "And now, as Oscar prepares to enter the ring, the crowd will be entertained with a recording of his recently released CD. It's a song called 'With These Hands.' Little does the crowd know they are listening to him singing a ballad about his boxing career. Of course, the lyrics are drowned out by the cacophonous crowd noise in the arena…" An indistinct flavor of dancy pop poured from the loudspeaker, while a montage of De La Hoya knocking out other boxers to hordes of screaming female fans projected across the overhead screen.

"Is this for real?" I asked Adam, nearly bursting out in laughter. The song, so romantic and out of place, swept along like the soundtrack of a nostalgic Hallmark movie.

"I told you. He's a rock star. Even if you don't like boxing, he can be another one of your pop-singer fetishes."

Adam had attempted to introduce me to *real* music like acid jazz and experimental rock, but I maintained an almost teenage girl–like addiction to the bad stuff.

When both boxers were in the ring, the cheering amplified to a roar. A man in a black tuxedo stood at the center and spoke into the microphone that hung from the ceiling.

"Introducing first, fighting out of the blue corner, wearing black with silver trim, and weighing in at 147 pounds, he brings a perfect professional record to the ring tonight...of 34 victories... Ladies and gentlemen, from Pomona, California...Suuuuuugar Shaaaaaaaane Mosleeeeeeeeey." The crowd's cheering was healthy but overshadowed by loud booing. Their discord made me want to root for him even more.

"And across the ring, fighting out of the red corner, wearing red-trimmed shorts with white letters and weighing 146 ½ pounds. His professional record stands at 32 wins with 1 loss... Ladies and gentlemen, from East Los Angeles...the Golden Boy, Oscarrrrrrr De La Hoooooyaaaaaa." The announcer listed all five championship belts and more titles and awards. The crowd went wild.

The bell clanged, and the fighters flew at each other, erupting in a series of punches, although I recognized no strategy. I had no idea how this boxing thing worked. Mosley smacked De La Hoya in the eye, immediately ruining his pretty face and speckling his forehead with blood. De La Hoya caught Mosley's gloves with his chest, abdomen and hips. Their bodies were quickly enveloped in sweat, which, when mixed with the Vaseline someone had slathered on them before the fight, made their gloves slippery and less effective.

"Oscar's gonna have to take the spin off the left jab and sorta point it at Shane Mosley, cuz if you spin it, you're gonna miss," George Foreman, one of the announcers, said. I recognized his name from a sandwich press Adam's grandmother had given us for Christmas one year. I loved the kitchen gadget, but I was surprised George also knew so much about boxing.

"Shane standing right in front of De La Hoya. Daring Oscar to try to stiffen him with his power. Now Mosley backs up and then comes straight forward again. Rips Oscar with a left hook. That's the speed of foot and hand. Embodied in one move." The announcers spoke in their own language, a kind of exaggerated, colorful word salad.

I closed my eyes and listened to the sounds: the crowd bustling, the corner men coaching, the announcers navigating. Even without looking at the screen, I could feel the energy of what was happening. The chaos held a rhythm, an order. I could see why this intricate brutality was popular in the Bronx. It gave meaning to pain and suffering.

When the bell rang again, the fighters retreated to their respective corners. An older man with a white goatee rubbed De La Hoya's face with a curved metal object and sprayed him with water. His trainer, according to the Spanish interpreter, was telling him not to go so hard and to use his jab. He stared straight ahead, emotionless.

In Mosley's corner, a man in a captain's hat rubbed his face with yet more Vaseline before moving to his shoulders. Mosley looked into his trainer's eyes, listening as he told him to continue with the right body shots and hit with the jabs. Then there was a replay of a particularly powerful hit to De La Hoya's ear, his head falling to the side like a Slinky. I cringed. The bell clanged for round two.

Each round continued like that: three minutes of fists flying, body shots and screaming fans, followed by thirty seconds of Vaseline rubdowns, cold metal and fervent instructions. I couldn't imagine the damage these men were incurring at the cellular level, but they kept coming back for more. By the fifth round, Mosley was behind and appeared to be struggling.

As a child I was never interested in sports. While my classmates enthusiastically attended basketball and hockey games, I begrudgingly dragged my flute to the bleachers to play with the band. I was only vaguely aware that teams were involved. Sunday nights were meant for *Charlie's Angels*, not perspiring men in tights and fancy halftime shows. In my family, the only acceptable team sport was eating, which we did with an almost competitive fervor. This was the first time a sporting event had meant anything to me. Maybe it was the simplicity of two men in a ring, or the fact that the rules differentiated it from the gang fights I cleaned up after in the hospital. But I suspected it was more than that. It was about the fighters themselves—who they were and what they stood for. It made me feel like I was part of something larger and more whole than myself.

Hours later and it was the twelfth and final round. Only crusts of pizza and the edge of a single black-and-white cookie remained. The fighters were tired, hanging onto each other between punches, resting in opposition. I couldn't tell who was winning or how they were winning. There was no knockout punch or dramatic fits of jabbing. But neither let up, both determined to bring everything they had to the ring. I envied them, their physicality, their bodies that allowed them that kind of physical expression.

The bell rang, signaling the end of the fight. There was a pause while everyone on screen milled around.

"What's happening?" I asked Adam, confused by the ending. I had expected something more dramatic.

"They're tallying up the points from the judges to see who won. It's gonna be close!" Adam was beside himself with excitement, pacing around the room and covering his lips with his fingers.

Tallying up the points? How could they give points for something so subjective? I tried to picture each judge keeping a mental scorecard, but it still made no sense.

The announcer was on the screen again. "And the winner, by split decision, is…Mosley!"

The crowd went crazy, cheering and booing and screaming at the same time. The sounds from the television echoed off the walls and spilled through the windows of our twelfth-floor apartment down to meet the fans, who were pouring out into the streets.

Mosley had won. But how? He didn't display any bravado or pound his opponent into the ground. He won slowly and steadily, using who he was as his strength instead of fighting it.

I hadn't considered that a strategy. Not once had I tried to be successful on my own terms. I just reacted to everything around me. As foreboding as it seemed, maybe it was time to let a little bit of myself out. Twisting and turning myself into what I thought I was supposed to be was no longer working. It was risky, but I had to find out who I really was. I was my last hope.

The next morning was Sunday, which meant hospital rounds started three hours later. On the way in, I passed my favorite orderly, who was seated on the steps in front of the hospital eating a meat pie. As he bit into the crust, oily red liquid dripped down the side of his face and landed on his name tag. *Rene.* With all the expletives I had made up for him in my head, I hadn't considered his real name—and an ambiguously gendered one at that. Heart pounding, I decided it was now or never.

"Hey, Rene, did you see the fight last night?" I asked, adding an extra lilt to my query.

He paused, opening his mouth just enough to display his half eaten bolus before he chewed and swallowed it down. "You watch da fight?" he asked, licking the oil off his lips, while his brain adjusted his opinion of me. "Dat Mosley has a mean right hook. I can't believe he won, mon."

Somehow, last night's words flowed out of me more easily than reciting the cranial nerves exiting the skull base. "De La Hoya tried to bring it, but losing to Felix Trinidad hit his confidence. And, as George Foreman says, 'You take that ghost into the ring with you, you may come out a ghost yourself.'"

"Ah, that's right. That's deep," Rene said, chuckling to himself. "You okay from the other day? I saw you run out front. Dat maggot guy really freak you out, huh?" The crooked edge of his mouth crept up the side of his face into a smile.

"Um, yeah. I almost puked," I said, admitting my weakness. But instead of shame, I felt relief. Whether I felt more feminine or more human, I couldn't decide, and it didn't matter. At that moment, I needed his kindness more than I needed my own contrived version of perfection. I was obviously onto something.

"Well, if you ever feel like you gonna puke again, you tell me. I help you clean it up," he said. He pursed his lips, furrowed his brow and nodded: the Bronx sign for *I've got your back.*

"Thanks, Rene." I beamed. "I'll keep that in mind."

4

I had long forgotten about boxing when it resurfaced.

By the end of residency, I had fully acclimated to the Bronx, handling gunshot victims and exsanguinating drug addicts like it was my actual job. Along the way I even picked up a few friends—like Ruby, the round ball of a desk clerk who traded sweet potato pies for my homemade cheesecakes, and Doug, the radiology supervisor who called me *Dahlicious* and made sure I never waited for a CT scan. When I walked away from my Wayne Avenue apartment, I was a fibrous mix of street smarts and sarcasm, with a soft underbelly reserved for my people. No longer the confused, frustrated intern of five years prior, I believed I was prepared for anything and everything that lay ahead. Little did I know that the Bronx was only round one.

As fate would have it, I was hired by one of the most elite practices on the Upper East Side. It happened, as many things do in this city, by timing and circumstance— a chance meeting with a private practitioner intrigued by hiring a female associate. Because women only accounted for 8 percent of practicing Ear, Nose and Throat doctors, I was just the unicorn they were looking for. Still, the probability of my procuring this job was as low as winning the lottery.

My tenuously held-together marriage was the first casualty, closely followed by loss of friends and familiar surroundings. Although I had made it out of the hood, the paltry income I earned as a new associate barely covered my Manhattan rent, let alone the expectations of that particular part of town. I was functionally no better off than I was at the beginning of residency. And that wasn't the worst part.

Of all the neighborhoods in New York, none have the affluence of the Upper East Side. Bounded by Ninety-Sixth Street to the north and Fifty-Ninth Street to the south, between Fifth Avenue and the East River, the Upper East Side contains the greatest concentration of individual wealth in the richest borough of the city and the most expensive real estate in the United States. It also had the highest concentration of physicians in the country. Of the seven hundred practicing Ear, Nose and Throat doctors in the entire state, two hundred of them were in my zip code. Although I had made it through the roughest time of my life, the fruits of my diligence were not yet ripe for the plucking. Surrounded by an ocean of social and medical elite, I was a plankton. And I barely knew how to swim.

★ ★ ★

"Dr. Marsh, is this your new associate? I heard you hired someone from the Bronx program, and I had to see her for myself." A middle-aged Indian man I didn't recognize approached us. His face, with large eyes bulging under highly concave lids and an openmouthed, permanent smile, reminded me of that Muppet on TV who always laughed at his own jokes. When he held out his hand to greet me, I was surprised there was no fur or invisible string. "I'm Dr. Patel. We've never met. I trained here, in the *city*," he said, emphasizing his geographic superiority.

This was the first holiday party I'd attended since joining the practice. My boss, Dr. Marsh, insisted I subject myself to more hospital functions to get to know my colleagues. Ten minutes in and it was already clear I didn't belong.

Dr. Marsh, at least twenty years my senior, was tall and lanky, with a white scruffy beard and glasses. He was detached and calm, yet somehow magnetic. His conversations easily drew people in, creating an intimacy that made even simple exchanges feel like shared secrets. He primarily treated children, and their parents loved him, as did every one of his colleagues.

I shook the moist and too-tight grip of Dr. Patel as he sized me up. I wanted to tell him not to worry because I was no match for him, especially in this hospital system. After residency, my colleagues scattered to other boroughs and the suburbs, so I had no connections in the city. But he seemed desperate to find that out for himself.

He introduced the woman standing next to him as his wife, a cardiologist. She wore enormous diamond earrings. I could barely make out her eyes from behind the reflection of her glasses, whose frame bore the interconnected Cs of affluence. She spoke slowly, waving her perfectly manicured fingernails in front of her face as her lips moved. "You must be new. Are you a resident? I usually know everyone at these functions, since we are so involved in the hospital." She looked me up and down, stopping with raised eyebrows at my neckline, which was obviously too low for her taste.

I slowly crossed my arms over my exposed chest, hating myself for yet again taking fashion advice from my mother. But I couldn't help it. Over the years, her criticism of my physical appearance had evolved into an art form, so convincing I believed in it like a religion.

When I had mentioned the party, she had insisted I buy a designer dress to impress the other doctors. To her, the word *designer* meant expensive and fancy, neither of which could be used to describe the black, V-neck Spice Girl's wardrobe malfunction she had found for me at TJ Maxx. Although she had pointed out that I was a little too old, fat and frumpy for the style, she had insisted I buy it anyway, reminding me I needed her guidance to learn how to be more feminine. According to her, my sense of style was only made worse by all those years of surgical scrubs and clogs, not that I had any idea how to look good before that.

In the sixth grade, my mother had decided I should get a haircut like Princess Diana. Instead of offering her usual homemade do, she had splurged on a cut at the expensive JCPenney salon. She had been convinced that flipped bangs and a shaggy bob would somehow make me prettier. At the very least, they would soften my harsh Arabic features. Once, when I had complained that a classmate had said my nose was uglier than my moustache, she had assured me there was no sense in thinking I would grow to love myself. "If you want to feel better," she offered, "you need to become a rich doctor so you can afford to fix your face."

"Uh, are you sure this will work with her hair?" the hairdresser had asked, lifting my coarse, wavy locks through spread fingers.

"Oh yes, her sister had that haircut last week, and it was perfect," my mother had insisted. My sister had the same delicate features and blond hair as my mother. In fact, she bore such little resemblance to me, people often questioned our relationship.

The hairdresser had gone to work, chopping away hair, trying to even out one side, then the other, until she could do no more. Literally. In the end, she'd left me with a Frankenstein-like crew cut. I was no Lady Di.

On the way home, my mother had tried to hide her horror. "You look mature," she said. "I'm sure no one else in your class has the same haircut." That part was true. The only children who had haircuts like mine were in military school.

The next day, I received the most attention I'd ever had in my life. At first I was proud. My father had told me if people stared, it meant they were jealous. It wasn't until lunch, when a first grader had pointed out to the whole lunchroom that I looked like the ugly duckling, that I realized what the stares really meant. I was a freak, and trying to be like everyone else made me stand out even more. I'd spent the rest of the day hiding in the bathroom, coming to terms with my place as a *darkie*, but still appreciative that my mother had tried to help.

One of the servers, wearing practically the same dress as me, carried a tray of drinks to where we were standing. I grabbed a glass and took a sip of the red liquid. "I haven't been in practice that long," I continued, wishing the wine could inebriate me on contact. "So, do you live in the city?" I asked, to no one in particular.

Dr. Patel could barely contain his excitement. My question set him up perfectly for his next segment. "Yes, we just bought in the Belvedere, a few blocks from here. The chairman of the board is my patient, so they approved us right away. Which is great, because our nanny has a shorter walk to our son's preschool. He goes to the Town School, with the granddaughter of the president of the hospital." He went on, dropping so many names and titles I wanted to offer him a suitcase to carry them home. "Where do *you* live?" he asked.

Quickly recalling his comments, I tried to piggyback

on some of them with my credentials. I had nothing. I
didn't have a nanny or know any chairs of any boards.
I didn't even know why knowing a chairman mattered
for an apartment. The Town School was apparently important for some reason, but I didn't know why a grown
man would care about preschool. And I didn't know any
presidents.

Since there was nothing even remotely impressive
about me, I chose a different strategy. I tried to be pur-
posefully vague. New York was so big I could just give
him a general area, and the questioning would stop. "I
live on York Avenue," I said and took another gulp of
wine.

He frowned, and his Muppet face instantly changed
to the grumpy one that looks like an eagle. "You mean
near the hospital? Those are great units." How was it
that he knew every single street and apartment building in the area?

"No, farther north. Ninety-First Street," I said, certain
he would be satisfied with that. Little did I know, he was
slowly giving me a rope long enough to hang myself.

"Oh, the Barclay. I know that rental," he said, visibly
relieved. "A lot of people start out there when they first
move to the city. It can take years to save up enough
to buy a place. I've been in practice close to seven, and
we've finally bought something."

"Yes, dear, but it's just the penthouse," his wife said,
tucking her hair behind her ear.

Seven years? We? Anywhere else in the country, my

salary alone would have been enough to buy a small mansion. In New York I was barely making it. After the divorce, I downsized to a one-bedroom near the projects so I could afford luxuries like utensils and sheets. My living situation was more college dorm than real home, eating leftover pizza on the floor until I could afford a couch. I was still waiting for the rich-doctor part to kick in, when my sacrifice and hard work would pay off. But from the sound of it, it wasn't happening anytime soon.

Pleased at my discomfort, Dr. Patel continued his line of questioning, moving on to a more personal subject. "So what does your husband do? Is he also a doctor?"

There was no way out of this one. I could either continue to try and weasel my way out or just buck up and take it. I remembered watching a movie about a guy who had to do a rap-off against a popular, more confident opponent. Every time he tried to battle, he choked and lost. In the final scene, he decided to own his own weaknesses up front, stealing the thunder from his opponent's rebuttal and winning the contest. I figured *What the hell?* I had nothing left to lose. It worked for Eminem, and he was from Detroit.

"I'm divorced," I said. "My husband was an artist who had even less money than me—can you believe it? I was lucky he even wanted to marry me. I mean, I grew up in North Dakota with crazy immigrant parents, so that doesn't exactly make you popular, you know? I trained in the Bronx, so I'm really good at dealing with gangsters and huge, fungating tumors, if you come across any of those. Needless to say, I don't know any chairmen or presidents of anything, but if you know any single ones, send them my way. I'd love to get out of my rental apartment." I uncrossed my arms, drained the last bit of wine and fought back the urge to mic-drop the empty glass.

Unfortunately, my words had the opposite effect I'd intended. Dr. Patel's expression changed to one of pity, suddenly aware that he'd wasted his arrows on such meager game. His wife grimaced and excused herself to use the powder room. Dr. Marsh shook his head and chuckled, enjoying the absurdity of the whole situation. He leaned in close and whispered, "Nice job."

I was just as awkward in the office. The practice I joined catered to the wealthy, and by *wealthy* I mean *ultra-rich*. Not like North Dakota, where *wealthy* meant you owned a Ford pickup truck with a second row of seats and your wall-to-wall-carpeted house wasn't in a trailer park. These patients owned things like grocery-store chains and small countries. I had known that the ultra-wealthy existed because I read about them in *Vogue* and the Style section of the *New York Times*. What I didn't know was that, by joining this practice, I would have to live and work among them in their native habitat. I felt like a zebra in a gilded jungle. And all the hyenas were dressed in Gucci.

"Good morning, Dr. Dahl. Your first patient is in room one. Dr. Marsh isn't in today, so we put Jimmy on your schedule. He's in there with his mom." Because I hadn't yet developed a following, the staff filled my schedule with overflows from the other doctors. It was hard to pick up where they had left off, but it was better than an empty schedule.

I read through the patient's chart. He was three years old and had persistent fluid in his middle ear. He also had speech delay, probably because the fluid muffled his hearing. Dr. Marsh had been treating him for six months, and today was just a follow-up. The stakes were low, but I still had a knot in my stomach. Even simple encounters were ripe with opportunities for humiliation.

Jimmy was seated on the exam chair in the lap of a woman who had the tan skin and dark hair of someone who came from the islands, possibly Puerto Rico, and spoke to him in Spanish. In the corner of the room, a blonde woman was focused intensely on a magazine I had never heard of. On the cover was a glossy picture of a model dressed in clothing no one actually wore.

"Hi, I'm Dr. Dahl. What can I do for you today?" That was my standard line, somewhere between flight attendant and telephone operator. Years working as a fast-food cashier in high school had permanently imprinted customer service into my psyche. It took everything I had to stop from asking if they wanted fries with their diagnosis. Without thinking, I looked straight up at the adult occupying the exam chair.

"That's Rosa, James's nanny. *I* am his mother," said the blonde, standing up in the tallest stilettos I had ever seen. Thick gold jewelry hung in strands from her neck and around her wrists. Her white pants were tight and unforgiving, but her body had nothing to beg forgiveness for. She looked at me through dull, expressionless eyes, pursing her artificially full lips before speaking. "*You* are the doctor?"

"Yes, I'm Dr. Dahl. Dr. Marsh isn't in today. I thought they'd explained that when they made your appointment." Although her face barely moved, she was visibly annoyed, I assumed because she was expecting to get what she'd paid for. My bosses took the paradoxical approach of charging cash up front for medical services. The way they explained it, when you are really rich, the more money you spend, the more elite the experience. To the very wealthy, it is more important to have something that no one else can afford than it is to have the best care.

She stared at me. "I wasn't expecting someone so… inexperienced. I hope you know what you're doing." She huffed and turned to pick up the child.

"No, no, no! Wosa, Wosa!" Jimmy screamed, squirming in protest and batting at his mother. As she reached for him, he lifted his arms, then went limp, using his dead weight to prevent the exchange of laps.

After thirty seconds of struggle and almost losing her balance, his mother finally relented. She took a step back and smoothed the edges of her hair again, nearly blinding me with the largest diamond I'd seen since Dr. Haven's.

Instead of making me angry like it had back then, it served more as a reminder of who was actually in charge.

"Okay, James. I know you're tired because we've been waiting so long for Dr. Dahl. You can sit there with Rosa," she said.

I glanced at the clock. It was only ten minutes after his scheduled appointment.

"Can I check your ears?" I asked Jimmy, slowly approaching him like a zookeeper circling a wounded animal. As I neared his head with my otoscope, he screamed and batted at me. Rosa impotently tried to calm him by patting his head.

"Can you hold his arms so I can take a look?" I asked, again misdirecting my question to Rosa.

His mother had returned to her seat in the corner, arms crossed. "I do not restrain my son," she said. "His therapist says it causes more anxiety. Strangers, like you, also make him nervous."

I was at a loss. I had to check him, but his mother was doing everything she could to reinforce my insecurity. I didn't know why she hated me so much, but her disapproval only made me want to impress her more.

"You really have no idea how to handle children. You're obviously not a mother. Did Dr. Marsh interview you himself, or did he let one of his lackeys hire you?" She shook her head, barely able to roll her eyes under heavy eyelids. Her skin was so smooth she looked like a talking sculpture with a horrible case of Botox. I wondered if the poison had leaked out of her face to her insides, freezing her heart like it had frozen her face.

Awkwardly, I grabbed the moving target of Jimmy's left ear and managed to peek inside with my otoscope. Behind his eardrum, the fluid had congealed into a glue-like substance that was unlikely to resolve unless I poked a hole through the membrane and drained it. In other words, surgery. I groaned internally, doubtful I had the courage to make that recommendation to his mother.

"Did you see anything?" she asked.

"Um, Jimmy still has fluid in his ears. He can't hear well, but if we remove the fluid his hearing will go back to normal." I ended the last syllable on a higher pitch, instantly transforming my statement into a question. I couldn't believe that, after all the hazing I'd endured in residency, I could still be so easily intimidated by this woman.

"You're saying you want to do surgery on my son? I told Dr. Marsh I don't believe in surgery! Didn't you read his chart?" I had read the chart, but Dr. Marsh hadn't written anything about how insane this mother was.

"James has been working with a homeopath. He's also getting acupuncture, speech and occupational therapy, and he has an aide in preschool. I can't believe your only suggestion is *surgery*! How can I be paying for this? I want to speak to the office manager!" She raised her voice so loud that the medical assistant peeked in to see if everything was all right.

Moving past the assistant, Jimmy's mother stormed

out of the room to the main desk, leaving me alone with Jimmy and Rosa. Both stared down at the floor, like prisoners in an invisible jail cell. Seeing that there was nothing left for me to ruin, I went to my office to hide.

Through the closed door, I could hear Jimmy's mother screaming about my incompetence, loud enough for the entire waiting room to hear. After what seemed like an eternity, her voice died down, and everything went quiet. There was a knock at the door.

"Come in," I said, my voice barely above a whisper.

It was Janet, the office manager. She was a tall woman in her fifties, who had worked for the practice for nearly a decade. I knew very little about her personal life, but her loyalty to the practice rivaled the fidelity in a solid marriage. She was direct about where everyone stood and didn't try to sugarcoat anything. "Well, she wasn't happy, but I managed to calm her down. I don't know what you did to her, but her husband runs a hedge fund and owns a lot of real estate on Park Avenue. I set up Jimmy to see Dr. Marsh later this week for a complimentary visit, but he won't be happy to hear about it."

In other words, I better learn how to behave, or my job would be in jeopardy. Any more mess-ups and Jimmy's mother would go down the street to another practice. And since the wealthy move in packs, she would take all her rich friends with her.

"I'm sorry. It won't happen again," I muttered. Those words felt too familiar. I'd spent half my life apologizing for what I didn't know instead of benefiting from what I did know. Ironically, moving from the Bronx to Manhattan had felt more like a step back than a step forward. Nothing I had learned from the hood helped me out in the jungle. I had to start all over again.

"Are you ready to go? Amber should be at the restaurant by now," Dr. Larson said, urging me out the door. He had been hired by the same practice a few months after me. Slight of stature and build, he carried himself with an air of entitlement. Other than the fact that we were around the same age and newly single, we had little in common. But he was the closest thing to a friend I had so far.

Amber was one of the drug reps. From what I understood, her job was to do whatever it took to get doctors to write prescriptions for the drugs she peddled. Most of the reps were female and stunningly beautiful. Sure, there were men in the sales force, but they were few and far between, selling serious drugs to seriously older doctors. Still, every rep had their own style. Some spouted off facts from research studies. Others disputed styles of medical treatment. Mostly, they just dressed provocatively and got us drunk at expensive dinners.

Dr. Larson and I were meeting another doctor for dinner, courtesy of Amber's employer. I knew little about him except that he practiced primary care a few blocks away, and Amber had said he was a good referral source. As specialists, we relied on referrals to grow our practices. Unlike doctors who worked for hospitals, in private practice we had to earn every single patient. Doctors rarely socialized without someone else footing the bill, so drug-rep dinners were how most relationships were made.

When we arrived at the restaurant, Amber and the other doctor were already seated at the table.

"I thought I was meeting two doctors tonight. Who is this young lady, Amber? Did your company hire a new rep?" the doctor asked, standing to shake my hand. He was in his early fifties, with a face so pudgy, he looked like he was having an allergic reaction to his nose.

"Oh, aren't you funny, Dr. Sheldon. This is Dr. Dahl. She works with Dr. Larson in Dr. Marsh's office." Amber flipped her hair back and rested her hand on her sternum, drawing his attention to where she wanted it. She wore a tight black suit, lacy camisole and pointy, patent leather heels. I had no idea how she walked around Manhattan all day like that. Even chunky heels hurt my feet.

Dr. Sheldon leaned in to Dr. Larson and said something under his breath. They both laughed, obviously sharing a private joke. "So you two have already met?" I asked, surprised at their familiarity. Amber had told me this was the first meeting for all three of us.

"Uh, yes, at, um, Robert's Steakhouse. There was a dinner last week," Dr. Sheldon said, giggling at his own words. He was already a dirty martini past tipsy and, by the look on Dr. Larson's face, sharing something that was supposed to have been a secret.

"I like steak," I said, surprised I hadn't been invited.

"Well, we weren't exactly eating steak," he said, winking and nudging Dr. Larson, whose face turned red. He was caught between sharing a moment with a new referral source and trying to hide the truth from me. We usually went to these dinners together, as a team, to represent our practice. I couldn't believe he was cheating on me.

Dr. Sheldon wouldn't stop talking. "*Robert's Steakhouse* is code for *Scores.*" He was laughing now, sticking his face into his martini glass to take another sip.

"You went to a strip club?" I asked, more upset at being excluded than by their choice of venue.

"Well, next time we'll bring you," Dr. Sheldon said, winking. His invitation made me feel even worse. I wanted to be part of the group, but the thought of watching my colleagues slobber over semiclad girls turned my stomach.

Appetizers and dinner came. The doctors talked about things I couldn't relate to, like golf clubs and expensive vacations. Dr. Larson cooed over his parents' favorite French Riviera resort, while Dr. Sheldon insisted his wife would only stay in Tuscany in the fall. I smiled politely and nodded, pretending I had visited such lavish locations. The town I grew up in was so small, my parents used to drive to Canada to show us what big cities looked like. Amber avoided the conversation altogether. She barely touched her dinner.

"You can just send me the check next week," Dr. Sheldon said, as we were leaving. "Hey, guys, make sure you write some prescriptions for Nasonase!" Nasonase was the drug Amber represented.

She took out a sheet of paper and laid it on the table. "Dr. Dahl and Dr. Larson, can I get your signatures please?" she asked. It was a sign-in sheet listing Dr. Sheldon as a speaker for a professional development lecture. Apparently, this dinner wasn't just about networking. I was beginning to see how doctors made it in this town.

"Dr. Dahl, I think we're going the same way. Can I walk you home?" Dr. Sheldon asked, his breath a humid cloud of tiramisu and alcohol. He swayed, trying to stand upright, leaning into me as he spoke.

I froze. I didn't want to go. Then, recalling my recent offense against Jimmy's mother, I realized I could no longer trust my instincts in this part of town. I rethought the situation. Dr. Sheldon was married, so obviously he wouldn't try anything. Even if he did, he was so drunk he posed little risk of following through. Alcohol is as unkind to blood flow below the belt as it is to the vestibular system. At the very least, helping the poor man home with dignity could get me a few more patients. Anything was better than seeing Dr. Marsh's overflow.

On the walk home, the night air was cool but dry. We strolled past meticulous townhouses with perfect shrubbery and apartment buildings with uniformed doormen. French restaurants glowed through curtained windows. Couples in Burberry and perfect hair strolled by arm-in-arm or pushed baby carriages of fraternal twins. From the outside, the Upper East Side looked like the perfect place to live.

Dr. Sheldon staggered a bit, leaning into me as we

walked so he wouldn't fall. The conversation was surprisingly disarming, discussing our mutual training programs and hometowns. He was impressed I'd made it so far from my humble beginnings, confessing he had never met anyone from the frozen north. It was nice talking to an older colleague about real things. I felt my guard drop a bit, exhausted from the night's pretenses.

"Do you mind if we stop by my office? I need to pick something up," he said, coming to a halt in front of a huge Park Avenue apartment building. A small sign affixed to a door just left of the main entrance displayed his name and credentials. I could see no reason why we shouldn't go in.

It was a typical New York doctor's office. The waiting area was small, the walls lined with eight padded wooden chairs and a plastic floor plant. A glass partition allowed access to the front desk, where a sign reminded patients that *Co-pays must be collected before the visit.* We walked past a magazine rack to his private office. Framed pictures of his wife and two teenage sons decorated the walls. Charts were arranged in a neat pile on a couch adjacent to his desk, which was empty except for a computer. He excused himself to go to the bathroom, so I sat in a chair across from his desk and waited.

"Do you want another drink?" he asked when he returned, sitting on the couch. He loosened his tie and leaned back into the large cushions.

"No, I've had enough. I have to operate tomorrow," I said, pitying his poor liver. I didn't start drinking until after my divorce, so my tolerance was pitiful. I could still feel the effect of my glass of Sancerre before dinner.

"That's nonsense. Why don't you come over here and sit next to me?" he asked, spreading his legs and patting the space next to him.

Suddenly realizing what was happening, I panicked. I had to get out of there, but there was no graceful way to do it. So I started talking. My mouth flooded with words, lots of words, nonsensical words, anything that would fill the time it took to make my way through his office and out the front door.

"Oh my God, is that the time? I'm so late, I'm such a lightweight, your office is so nice, I have to call my mom, thank you so much, you are so sweet, is that a real plant? I have to go..."

I ran home, swimming through the evening's events in my mind, desperate to see where I had gone wrong. I couldn't make any sense of it. He was married and old, and we worked in the same hospital. If he'd got his wish, it wasn't like we could avoid each other. Or maybe that was how it worked on the Upper East Side. Had Amber known he was planning to seduce me? Maybe this was how the referral system really worked, and she was trying to help me out. It was probably my fault, but how had I misled him? I thought I was *supposed* to be nice. My head was spinning. I suddenly missed the Bronx, my husband, Rene and even Jerome. At least they were familiar. Not like this place. The Upper East Side made the Bronx seem like an inconvenient road stop on the way to actual hell. But unlike the Bronx, my current location had no end date.

At work the following week, it was back to the grind. Overflow patients and the occasional referral dotted my schedule—none from Dr. Sheldon. One afternoon, starving for lunch, I had one more patient to see before my break. Little did I know, my burger would be cold and dry by the time I got to it.

"Uh, you're the doctor? Nice!" the patient said as I walked in. "My name's Ned." His toupee was thick and chocolate brown and obviously not his own hair. It crowned his deeply furrowed brow and extended in outstretched arms, reaching for his sideburns. His beard and moustache were peppered white. Relaxing in folds against his neck, his chin disappeared beneath a black high-collared turtleneck.

"What can I do for you?" I asked, still with the fast-food routine.

"Well, let me see," he thought, a little too hard, and scrolled through his mental Rolodex of ailments. "I have this drip. It's nothing, really, just gets annoying. I mean, otherwise I'm really healthy. I'm a young guy, I work out, love dancing…"

"So, how long have you had this postnasal drip?" I interrupted, remembering a technique we learned in medical school called *directing the patient*. It was the technical term for cutting off the ones that were obviously going to drone on about their symptoms and therefore waste precious face time.

"The drip? I've had it forever. I mean, it doesn't really bother me. Mostly happens after I eat. Well, and sometimes when I wake up in the morning. But I usually go for a workout right away, so it doesn't bother me much after that…" He moved his hands in small karate chops with each statement.

I tried again. "Do you have any allergies? Any inhalants or dust at work?" He was testing my patience. My stomach let out a high-pitched whine of hunger that we both ignored.

"No allergies. I'm really healthy. I'm not working now, so I spend a lot of time in Florida. I have an apartment there. But I used to be a producer for HBO sports, like *Boxing after Dark* and stuff like that."

The mention of boxing jolted me out of my inertia like a clapper against the inside of a bell. "Wait, you worked at the fights?" Boxing was a distant memory, conjuring flashes of Saturday night fights in the Bronx. Pizza and black-and-white cookies. Mosley and De La Hoya. Screaming crowds and tuxedoed announcers. Rene, the orderly, and his greasy meat sandwich.

"Sure, that was one of my regulars. You a boxing fan?" He raised his brow in surprise, his toupee lifting at the center, inadvertently exposing adhesive.

"Yes, I am. I mean, I was. When I was in residency." I thought back. Compared to the island of isolation that was my current existence, that time seemed like a vibrant community. Lost in thought, I remembered something, a tiny memory I had forgotten until that very moment.

During my fourth year, I was on call one night with the neurosurgery resident, Sam. We were in the ICU, checking on a patient who was intubated and unconscious. Amid the din of beeping and clicking wires and tubes, I heard the faint but familiar sounds of a crowd cheering. I looked up from the patient's tracheotomy and noticed a tiny television suspended from the wall behind the bed. The arm attached to it had been swiveled so the television faced his closed, comatose eyes. Curious, I rotated the screen to see two boxers hanging on to each other, sweat pouring down their faces. Moments later, the bell clanged, and they took to their corners. At the edge of the screen, a man in a suit squatted next to one of the boxers, leaning in to check a cut.

"Who's that guy?" Sam asked. He had moved from the head of the bed and was standing behind me, holding a syringe of bloodied fluid in his gloved hands.

"I have no idea," I said, confused by the suited man's formality. His movements were robotic and awkward. He didn't seem to belong there.

"He's wearing latex gloves. Is that the cut man?" Sam asked.

Before I could speak, the announcer answered for me. "And here we have the doctor...checking Torres...to see if that cut is nasty enough to stop the fight."

"They have doctors in boxing? Wow. I bet that would be a cool job. Hell, with the kind of training we get here, we could do that with our eyes closed," Sam said, shrugging and turning back to the patient. He squirted the liquid into a kidney basin and re-inserted the needle into a soft spot on the patient's head, where his team had removed a piece of cranium.

I watched as the doctor nodded to the referee. As he climbed out of the ring, I considered what had just happened. With the thousands of screaming fans, fighters, promoters and judges, this mousy guy got to decide if the fight could go on. That was power, the likes of which I had never known.

I was reveling in that notion, feeling it swell and expand in my chest, when my mouth formed the words that would forever change my life. "I want to be a fight doctor."

Ned tilted his head to the side, considering my statement, then brightened. "I can make some phone calls for you. My friend knows Teddy Atlas." He pursed his lips and nodded his head slowly. "The boxing commission would love you. They don't have any lady fight doctors, especially not from this part of town." I didn't know who Teddy Atlas was or why my being a woman mattered, but he seemed to be taking me seriously.

"Yeah, that sounds good," I said, unsure of the implications. He probably wouldn't even follow through.

"Do you want me to come back for a follow up? I don't want any medicine or anything. I just wanted you to check to make sure everything's okay." He could tell

I was no longer paying attention to him. It was his turn to direct the doctor.

"Uh, sure. Come back in a month," I said, embarrassed of my momentary lapse into the past.

"Perfect. I'll have some news on that boxing gig by then, too," he said, shaking my hand.

Watching him walk toward checkout, toupee firmly in place, I pondered the significance of his visit. Whether it was just a reminder of what I had left behind or an omen for the future, I wasn't sure. But I couldn't wait to find out.

5

If life is a painting in progress, then hope is that unfinished space in the background. My hope was still beige, the color of faded muslin—full of potential, but dulled from anticipation. Nine months after I had filled out the application, there was still no word from the commission. Tired of waiting, I surrendered to the monotony of my immediate circumstances: thirty-five patients a day, more drug-rep dinners and the occasional hospital function. I was digging out a thick ball of earwax when I finally got the phone call—freeing the sticky substance at the very moment boxing came to free me.

"Hi, this is Sally from the Athletic Commission," a woman with a perky voice said over the phone. "I've got your first fight assignment."

"An assignment? Already?" I was confused. How could they give me an assignment when they hadn't even interviewed me? There had to be a mistake.

"Yeah, it's says here Dr. Williams, the Chief Medical

Examiner, approved you. You're listed as one of the doctors for the next fight."

I was shocked. How could this Dr. Williams approve my appointment without meeting me? Medicine didn't work that way. There were interviews and more interviews, exams and waitlists. The surprise made me more suspicious than happy, but I wanted to let it play out. "That's great! I can't wait to get started," I said, suffocating my instincts.

"Great! You just gotta show up at the venue—"

"Wait. Just like that? Isn't there anything I can read beforehand?" I asked, my pulse rising. I knew nothing about being a fight doctor. I didn't even know the rules of boxing. And I hadn't seen a fight since Tyson had ripped Holyfield's ear off with his teeth.

"Read? Ha ha, no. You just kind of learn as you go. Don't worry, the other guys won't let you get into any trouble." She laughed, as if my question was the most ridiculous thing she'd ever heard.

She had to be wrong. Everything in medicine involved a textbook or training manual. Wasn't there a guy who wrote a book about being a fight doctor? Freddie something? I would obviously have to figure that part out myself. "Uh, okay. Ha ha ha," I said, feigning laughter. "Where's the fight?"

"You will be—" she paused, fumbling through some papers "—working the Gerry Cooney Charity fight at the New York Hilton. It's next Thursday, October fourteenth."

When I had turned in my application, I'd pictured my first fight in a dark, sweaty ring somewhere in the

Bronx. I didn't know a fight could even be held in a hotel. Didn't they need a ring? And who was this Gerry Cooney guy? If it was a charity event, did that mean I had to dress fancy? How would I get in and out of the ring in a ball gown? I had questions, but I feared exposing my ignorance.

"This may sound silly, but what should I wear?" I asked, nonchalantly.

"Well, I wouldn't wear anything light-colored," she said gruffly. "It'll just get covered in blood."

I was relieved. Blood I could handle. And my closet was full of dark suits that could easily tolerate the dark stain of hemoglobin.

"The fight is Thursday night," she continued, "so come to the commission at 5:00 p.m. on Wednesday to do the weigh ins and prefight physicals."

Would the madness never cease? The limits of my specialty ended at the clavicles, which meant I hadn't done a full physical since internship. I thought back to my gross anatomy class in medical school, hopeful that cutting apart a pickled human, sinew by sinew and nerve by nerve, had burnt some of those landmarks into my brain.

"You're sure there isn't a manual?" I asked once more, hoping there was some beat-up rule book to at least get me started.

"Aw, you'll be fine," she said warmly. "See you at the fights." She gave me the address to the commission headquarters and hung up.

What had I gotten myself into? I had been so sure this

boxing thing wouldn't come through, I hadn't bothered to prepare. Instead of feeling excited, I was worried. It wouldn't take them long to figure out I was a fraud. I would probably end up confessing it myself because it was the right thing to do. I had always been terrible at accepting unearned gifts.

When I was in high school, a friend and I had planned a party. Pooling our money together, we bought the biggest bottle of 190-proof Everclear we could find. Wanting to stretch the limits of our alcohol, we lined a jumbo garbage can with a Hefty bag and poured in the alcohol with enough juice and diced fruit to get twenty-five teenagers drunk. Halfway through our boozy punch, the party was raided by local police. Terrified, I ran to the back of the apartment, found an open window and climbed through.

Standing alone outside the apartment, I realized I was free. While the rest of my classmates were lining up for punishment, I could walk away and pretend the whole thing had never happened. But instead, I panicked. Unable to handle my good fortune, I made my way back inside, through the same open window, to get my hundred-dollar summons like everyone else.

Maybe I didn't have to repeat that mistake again. I had spent too much time earning rewards and not enough time collecting them. Since hard work alone wasn't paying off, I wanted to see how good luck felt.

Wall Street was not a part of town I frequented. The oldest part of the city, it was built chaotically, like a toddler let loose with a box of Legos. The streets were tiny and winding, barely wide enough for modern cars. Scaffolding shadowed the narrow sidewalks. People had to move in near single file to get anywhere. Turning onto William Street, I had trouble finding the address of the New York State Athletic Commission among the tall glass buildings. It wasn't until I noticed a small huddle of men in puffy jackets and baseball caps, completely out of place next to the Armani suits, that I knew where to go.

After showing my ID to the security guard, I rode alone up to the nineteenth floor. The elevator opened to a large crowd gathered in the lobby of the commission headquarters. A hodgepodge group of casually dressed men were chatting quietly. I counted only one other woman. This crowd could have easily come from any street corner in the Bronx. It felt like home.

"You must be Dr. Dahl," said a lanky man who seemed to appear out of nowhere. He looked like he was in his early thirties, staring at his clipboard as he spoke without making eye contact. When I didn't answer, he looked up with a blank expression. "I'm Tom Marino. I'll show you where you'll be doing the physicals."

I followed him through the crowd into an empty classroom, where desk chairs were lined up in rows facing the front of the room. The walls and floors were worn like an inner-city high school. At a large table at the front, a man was browsing through a manila folder. He had chestnut skin and dark hair that was slicked back into a hirsute helmet.

"This here is Dr. Gonzalez. Dr. Gonzalez…Dr. Dahl. Here's some more files. I'll come back with the rest later." Tom rested a pile of folders on the table before leaving the room.

Dr. Gonzalez smiled broadly. Powdery men's cologne rose from his gray, sharkskin suit. The shiny material, along with his light blue shirt and iridescent tie, made him look like he had just strutted out of a men's magazine.

"Hey, hey, hey! You must be the newbie. Welcome! Looks like they're pairing you up with the old fart," he said. He was clearly around my age, so I didn't understand the comment.

"Old fart? What are you talking about? You're younger than me," I said, figuring it would be a compliment either way.

"Oh, I've been around awhile. What's it been…maybe four years? I started in residency, so, you see. Old fart." I didn't really see. But, remembering that all doctors are trapped in the hierarchy of our respective training programs, he was probably just trying to show me he had been around longer. That made him more senior, regardless of our actual ages.

"You're ENT, right?" he asked but, before I could answer, pointed at himself. "Pain management."

"Is that what you call yourself?" I asked, assuming he was explaining the job description of a fight doctor.

"I'm in Pain Management up at Columbia. Kind of appropriate, right?" He laughed at his wittiness and shrugged his shoulders. Even with his posturing and fancy suit, I found him charming.

We continued our conversation, which was mostly him explaining his résumé and why he had more fight assignments than any other commission doctor. "I'm just a sucker for a good fight. Plus, they know I'm always available. My wife gives me a long rope," he said, dangling a make-believe one from his neck. I listened, sharing as little as possible about myself. I didn't care about accolades. I was just happy to be there.

The first boxer interrupted our conversation. His eyes were hidden behind Dolce and Gabbana sunglasses, under a hat that read *New York* in rhinestone cursive letters. Sweaty and out of breath, his small frame was wrapped in a red warm-up suit and cloaked with more clothing. He took his place in the chair next to me.

"Tyrone, right?" Dr. Gonzalez asked. "This is Dr. Dahl. She's new to the commission. I'm just gonna have her watch me do some physicals before we let her loose on her own." Then he turned to me and dangled a reflex hammer between his first and second fingers. "I'll bet you haven't used one of these in a while," he said, spinning it around like a baton. He was right about that.

He turned back to Tyrone, suddenly assuming an authoritative tone. "Take off your glasses. We'll do the neuro exam first cuz it's the hard part. Looks like you didn't make weight." I wondered how he knew that.

"Nah, man. Two pounds over. I'm sweatin' it out." That would explain the outfit and perspiration. He was already thin. I couldn't imagine what he would look like two pounds lighter.

"Well, I hope your brain's not too dehydrated. It's time for the neuro exam!" Dr. Gonzalez laughed at his own hilarity. He glanced at Tyrone and me and, seeing that his audience wasn't amused, went back to his serious face. "Okay. These questions may seem a little strange, but I want you to answer them to the best of your ability.

"What is the date?"

"Uh, Wensdee," said Tyrone, eyes closed.

"Day of the week and time to the nearest hour. With-*out* looking at the clock."

"October thirteenth, uhhhh, I think it's, uhh, around five o'clock? I's hungry, G," he whined, glancing up at an older man who was standing against the wall. He offered no help, shaking his head and looking away.

"Now on to the harder stuff," Dr. Gonzalez said, ignoring Tyrone's complaint. "I'm gonna give you five words, and you have to repeat them back to me. And remember them cuz I'm gonna ask for them again at the end. Okay? Here they are: *Table. Red. Apple. Pen. House.*"

"Tayble…rayud…payun…hayouse…apple?" he slurred. Tyrone struggled with the words, pronouncing even the one syllable words with two syllables. "We almos' done?" He was getting agitated.

"Not quite. Now I want you to name the months of the year backwards, starting with December."

"Sheeut. How's I s'posed to know that?" Tyrone shifted in his chair, rolling his eyes and shaking his head. His cheeks were sunken so deep into his skull I could see its outline. He looked more like a malnourished cancer patient than an athlete.

"Just try," Dr. Gonzalez said. "I know you're tired."

"Decembah...uh...Novembah...Octobah...September-bah...uhhhh..." Then, in a whisper, "Janary, Febury, March, April, May, June, July, August," and back to a louder voice, "August...July..." He went back and forth like that until he successfully arrived at *Janary*. Then he sighed. "Man, *why* you gotta ask this stuff? What's it got to do with boxing?" I was wondering the same thing. Questions like that were usually reserved for psychiatric and stroke patients.

"Just answer the questions," Dr. Gonzalez said, un-fazed. I wanted to get Tyrone some water or a Big Mac or something, but I didn't dare move. This felt more like the entrance exam.

"Now, what were those five things I told you before? Do you remember?" Dr. Gonzalez was animated now, looking hard into Tyrone's eyes, like he was trying to give him the answers through telepathy.

"What? Oh, sometin' bout a rayud apple in a hayouse?" I was surprised he remembered any of the words. I had already forgotten all of them.

"Well, actually—" Dr. Gonzalez made a stern expres-sion, then broadened the corners of his lips into a huge smile "—you passed! Congratulations!"

He leaned over to me and whispered, "That test is just to make sure they're not too brain damaged to fight.

They set the bar pretty low, but you'd be surprised how many guys fail." I was wondering if even I could have passed, especially with so little food and water.

"Now on to the easy part, Tyrone. Strip down to your pants." I looked around for a changing room, but there was only open space. Tyrone didn't seem to care, peeling off his clothes, layer by layer until he was nearly naked. His body was lean and muscular, with no discernible fat.

Dr. Gonzalez began his exam. He did a quick inspection of Tyrone's ears and mouth and listened to his chest with a stethoscope, muttering the word *good* with each element, like he was completing his own mental checklist before he filled out the hard copy.

"Now stand," he said, grabbing Tyrone's forearm and pushing against it. "Resist me." Even though Dr. Gonzalez was clearly better fed and leaning in with his entire body weight, Tyrone easily pushed back. When Dr. Gonzalez switched to the other arm, I noticed a large square discoloration that covered most of Tyrone's left bicep.

"Did you get burned?" I blurted out before remembering my place. Dr. Gonzalez stiffened and glanced over at me.

"Yeah. In the fourth grade. Third degree. I was playing near my gramama's stove."

"Did you have a skin graft?" I asked. I didn't know a lot about burns, but I remembered the burn unit as the saddest place in the hospital.

"Nah. Gramama didn't believe in doctors." He looked back at Dr. Gonzalez. "Can we finish this?"

I was horrified. The thought of recovering from that kind of injury without pain medication or medical care almost made me sick. He must have had to disconnect from his physical body for survival's sake. No wonder he was a boxer.

Dr. Gonzalez, unaffected by this new bit of medical history, continued his exam. "Walk heel-to-toe along this line. Good. Now turn around, close your eyes and put your arms straight out. Yeah, like that. Now hop twenty times on each foot." After Tyrone finished the exercise, Dr. Gonzalez took his pulse. "Sixty beats per minute. You're in excellent shape, dude. Get dressed."

As Tyrone fumbled for his clothes, I studied the rest of his upper body. "What about that one, there?" I asked, pointing at an irregular, thick, three-inch scar on his right shoulder.

"Dat's from the tird grade," he said, looking at it and shrugging. "I's bored."

"And that one?" I asked, spotting a group of thick keloids across his abdomen.

"Gangbanger went at me with a knife." He glanced sheepishly at his manager and put his shades on. I thought of my old patient Jerome and, for the first time, wondered what had become of him.

"We done now?" he asked, edging toward the door.

"Yeah, we're done," Dr. Gonzalez said. "Go see if you made weight, and get something to eat. See you tomorrow night."

"He has more injuries from his life than he does from

boxing," I said, disturbed by what I had seen. I was used to seeing people in the immediate aftermath of their injuries. I hadn't thought about what happened to them when and if they left the hospital.

"Funny, I never usually notice scars and burns and things like that. If I did we'd be here all night. These guys have messed-up bodies. We mainly look for brain injuries, bad vision and hand trauma. *Those* are the things that affect their ability to fight." It seemed to me he had it backwards. The scars were probably what made them want to fight in the first place. I wondered if this job would make me lose my compassion, too.

He continued. "It's kind of silly. The fighters have to do the weigh ins the night before the fight, then they just go home and eat everything they can. Their actual fight weight is probably five pounds over. No one's figured out a better way to do it, so it is what it is. Let's go through the paperwork."

He sat at the table and flipped through the rest of the chart. "They have to get yearly HIV and hepatitis checks, EKGs and eye exams. Every three years they need an MRI. You'd think that neuro exam would be enough!" he said, yet again attempting to make me laugh.

I wasn't appreciating the humor, so I tried to help him out. "I guess it makes sense to check for STDs. They share some of the same bodily fluids as porn actors, right?" Years of surgical training had made my dark sense of humor even darker.

"Ha ha, yeah," he said, looking at me with renewed

interest. "You are a cool chick. I think you're really gonna like this."

"I'm Dr. Roy," another man said, extending his hand as he entered the room. "Nice to meet you." He was several years older than Dr. Gonzalez. More subdued, he had already removed his tweed jacket and was rolling up his sleeves when he introduced himself. "Has Dr. Gonzalez been showing you the ropes?"

"That's funny," I said, acknowledging the pun. He had the natural cool Dr. Gonzalez seemed so desperate for. I liked him already.

"Now that you've seen a physical, are you ready to do one on your own?" he asked, grabbing a manila folder and scanning the contents.

"Sure," I said, completely unsure. But there was a big pile of charts, and I wanted to be useful.

"Great. Here's Juan. You can check him in. He's been through this enough times he can probably do it himself," he said, patting Juan's enormous shoulder.

Juan was much taller and thicker than Tyrone. Although I didn't yet know the weight classes, I could tell he was a heavyweight.

"Hi, *mami*," Juan said, bowing his head and removing his hat. *Mami*. I hadn't heard that word since I'd left the Bronx. I remembered when Rene first called me *mami*, a term of endearment that I initially mistook as an insult. What used to make me so angry now warmed my heart with its familiarity. When I lived in the Bronx, I couldn't wait to get out, but now I had more in common with the people there than the Upper East Side. We were just speaking different languages.

I fumbled through his chart. He was twenty-eight years old and had a record of ten wins and five losses. His labs and tests were all normal except for his vision—twenty-twenty in one eye and twenty-forty in the other. "Is this okay?" I asked Dr. Gonzalez, who had moved on to another fighter.

"Yeah, close enough," he said. "It's not rocket science. They just have to be able to see their opponent without contact lenses or glasses. Can't fight with either of those."

Juan made it through the neuro exam quickly, beating me to the answers before I asked the questions. His brain was obviously working just fine.

"Okay, Juan, you can remove your…" Before I could finish my sentence, he had already undressed down to his sweatpants. He was tall, over six feet two, and towered over me. Surveying his thick muscles, I had no idea how I was going to be able to push hard enough to test his strength. But the competitive side of me was going to try anyway.

"Resist me," I said, grasping his forearm and leaning back with my entire bodyweight. The irony of my request didn't escape me. Although I was thankful I could finally put my thickness to good use, I felt more like I was flirting than doing a physical exam. Missing the humor entirely, Juan easily pushed back, almost knocking me down.

"Oh, sorry, *mami*," he said, helping me up. Despite my

embarrassment at falling, I loved that he was so physically powerful. It was like wrestling a grizzly bear I knew wouldn't hurt me.

"No, it's okay. Let's keep going," I said, suppressing my inner monologue to regain composure. I continued the exam, nearly falling over each time I pushed or pulled at one of his limbs. But I appreciated the dance. I was so used to feeling like I had to be the strongest person I knew it was a relief to be with someone stronger.

After seven more physicals, we finished checking in all the fighters.

"See you tomorrow night at the fights," Dr. Roy said. "And remember—don't wear high heels. You may trip climbing into the ring."

I had never heard of Gallagher's Steakhouse but, when Tom called to invite me to dinner with the commission before the fight, I gladly accepted. Passing an open-display meat locker at the front entrance, I walked into the restaurant and past the bar. It was old-school New York, all dark wood and leather and last night's smoke, with framed pictures of celebrities covering the walls. The place was empty except for a cluster of small tables in the back, where seven men were seated. Relieved of the confines of their daily work life, some had removed their jackets and rolled up their sleeves. Others had loosened their ties so they hung like open nooses around their necks. I recognized Dr. Gonzalez, who was just as fastidiously put together as the night before.

"You must be Dr. Dahl. I'm David," a man said, standing and offering his hand. He was mostly bald, with a patch of gray hair around the periphery of his head. His face, which was once undoubtedly handsome, had aged into wrinkled skin and a bulbous nose. Almost disturbing in their clarity, his blue eyes glowed even brighter through his tan skin. His expression was remarkably innocent for a man of his age and position.

"David John Jacobs? The commissioner?" I asked, hoping I had remembered his name correctly. I wanted to make a good impression, and I couldn't wait to thank him. He was one of the men who had made it all happen.

"Well, there are a few commissioners, but I'm the chairman. Have a seat," he said, pointing at the chair nearest him. "Meet everyone else: Johnny, Ralphie, Mikey, Jerry, and you know Tom and Fred Gonzalez." He gestured around the table, introducing each man with a wave of his hand. I felt like I was with the Godfather and he was introducing me to his Dons.

I smiled at the table and took my seat next to the Chairman, saying nothing. I knew I wouldn't remember their names so I didn't bother trying.

"We already ordered. Whaddya you want?" the Chairman asked, leaning in to me.

"Anything is fine," I said. I hadn't eaten since breakfast and hoped someone had ordered appetizers. There was no bread at the table, and I was starving.

"What?" he asked, squinting and moving in closer. "Do you want steak?" he asked, in an even louder voice.

"Yes, thanks," I said, with as much volume as I could stand to hear in my own voice. He stared intently at my mouth, straining to hear.

"I haven't seen you around, Dr. Dahl. Are you a big fight fan?" asked one of the men, Johnny or Mikey, studying me through suspicious eyes. His shirt, stained with grease near the collar, was unbuttoned to the top of his sternum. Strands of thick, black hair peeked out, hinting at the forest that grew beneath.

"Yes, actually. I used to watch it a lot when I was in residency in the Bronx."

"So, you've never actually been to a fight? That's funny. Usually the docs watch a lot of fights. Gonzalez here started when he was a student."

"I was a resident, not a student," Dr. Gonzalez said, peevishly. "I've been doing this for four years, man. How have I put up with you guys for so long?" He forced a laugh and shook his head, trying to be one of the guys, but failing to be one of *these* guys.

"What kind of doctor are you, Linda? Can I call you *Linda*?" The eldest, most distinguished-looking man, spoke next. He sat across from me, wearing glasses and sporting a gray, neatly cut beard. His interlaced fingers rested on the table in front of him, like he was about to start an inquisition. I was so nervous I couldn't remember which name was his, but he clearly knew mine.

"I'm an ENT. Actually, with all the cuts and nose-bleeds, I should come in handy," I said, trying to direct his questions toward my useful skill set and away from my ignorance.

"I guess. Never thought of it that way." He took a sip of ocher liquid from his glass and continued the interrogation. "Where do you practice?"

"I'm part of a group on the Upper East Side," I said, for the first time feeling a sense of pride about that, too. He seemed surprised, but not nearly as surprised as Dr. Gonzalez, whose jaw dropped in disbelief.

"My doctor practices up there, too. He's with Presbyterian—Dr. Goldstein. Do you know him?" He was testing to see if I really was who I said I was. But there was more to it. He was also trying to figure out why a doctor like me, who worked in such a prestigious part of town, would want to work at the fights. I knew there was no way he would understand.

"I've heard of him, but we've never met," I said. It was a lie, but not really. I didn't know his exact doctor, but in my zip code of 5,000 of us, at least three were called Dr. Goldstein. "How are you involved in the fights? Are you a judge?" I asked, trying to cross-examine my prosecutor.

"Ha ha, no. I have no interest in that. I'm a commissioner for the state," he said.

Before I could clarify what that meant, Johnny/Mikey interrupted. "So, I still don't get it. Didn't anyone interview you? How do you even know what you're doing?"

I wanted to cry. He'd exposed my fraudulence in front of everyone, and I had no defense. But he also confirmed what I had suspected: that my immaculate conception into the world of boxing was just that. I was a true virgin.

Then, like a miracle, the Chairman rescued me. "Well, we're glad to have you. You're the only woman on the panel, and I'm sure you'll do a great job."

I audibly exhaled, suppressing tears of relief. "Hopefully, I can learn a lot and do a good job," I said, thankful.

The servers came with the food, setting a small plate in front of each of us that held a single cut of steak. There were no plates of fries or creamed spinach, no baskets of bread. Just meat. I looked around the table at what we were: a tribe of urban warriors about to devour our kill before the next battle.

6

The New York Hilton is a four-star hotel located up the street from Rockefeller Center, in the geographical center of Manhattan. Sandwiched between Times Square to the west and Midtown to the east, it is a crossroads of chaos and restraint. Huddles of overdressed tourists in unreasonable shoes obstruct the flow of businessmen marching into an angry void. Arabic music plays from halal trucks, where immigrants cook sweaty meat across the street from five-star restaurants. It was a strange place in its own right, but an even stranger place to hold a boxing match.

Riding the escalator to the basement of the Hilton with my group, I realized I had to devise a game plan for the night. Thanks to Johnny/Mikey, everyone knew I was a complete rookie as a fight doctor. But what I didn't want them to discover was how little I knew about boxing in general. As luck would have it, Johnny/Mikey split off from the group early. With him gone, I decided to use a tactic I learned early in med school: feigned understanding.

I was first exposed to this effective tool during my general surgery rotation. My friend Amy and I were students on the team, and only one of us could scrub in for surgery at a time. This particular case was of the open bowel variety, one that would involve hands-on experience—a rare and precious opportunity for a student.

The attending turned to me first, asking me to recite branches of the abdominal aorta. I was caught off guard, having wrongly prepared to discuss the specifics of colon cancer, the reason for surgery in the first place. Unseasoned in the art of pimping, I muttered the three most cursed words in surgery: *I don't know.* In light of my incompetence, Amy was chosen for the case.

I stood back and watched as she brilliantly navigated through her parallel ignorance. When the attending screamed, "Suck in the hole, suck in the hole!" she didn't ask which hole or when, she just stuck the suction in the most recent one and nodded. When he asked her to list the causes of colon cancer, instead of admitting she had no idea, she commented on the brilliance of his tumor excision. Jealously watching her cut sutures as he reattached the bowel, I promised myself that, when it came to anything medical, I would never again admit to what I didn't know.

If I wanted to learn anything tonight without humiliating myself, I, too, would have to be brave in my stupidity. I would have to sponge up every sensory clue around me to present some semblance of understanding.

"Let's start in the back. Some of the fighters are here, so we can check them in," Dr. Gonzalez said when we got downstairs. He led me into an enormous conference room, identical to those used for medical seminars. The ring had been set up in the center, surrounded by folding chairs and banquet tables. It was smaller than I had imagined, dwarfed by the size of the room. A few people dressed in black milled around, assembling camera equipment and sound cables. It looked more like a movie set than what I was used to seeing on television.

I followed Dr. Gonzalez to a curtained area, where small groups of men were seated. He found an open space and set down his bag, emptying its contents onto an adjacent table. Picking up a stethoscope, he hung it around his neck like jewelry. I made a mental note to keep track of his other tools as the night went on so I could gather my own stash before the next time. If there was a next time.

"We have to do a quick check of the boxers on the day of the fight," he said, beginning his preview of the night. "Then, they have to go with Charlie over there—he's one of the inspectors—so he can watch them pee in a cup." I looked over at a heavyset man, standing with his arms held rigidly against his sides.

"The urine check is to make sure there are no drugs in their system," I said, stating what I assumed was true instead of asking the question.

My comment had the magical effect of making Dr. Gonzalez feel like he had to show me up, feeding me more details to fill in the gaps of what I didn't know. "Yes, right. The pee cup also has a plastic thermometer on the side so you can tell the temperature. That way the fighter can't pour water in there or use someone else's urine."

The thought of someone carrying around a vial of stolen urine made me laugh. I wondered if there was a black market for untainted pee.

"Look, there's Tyrone," he said. A young man who was too hale to have been the same fighter as the night before sat on a folding chair, sharing a joke with the man next to him. He looked almost healthy, face plump and eyes bright. If Dr. Gonzalez hadn't pointed him out, I wouldn't have recognized him.

"Looks like you got something to eat, dude," Dr. Gonzalez said, echoing my sentiment.

"Yeah, Madonna's, man. Lotsa meat!" He said the word *meat* with a guttural sound, loud and throaty, as if he had killed it himself.

"Madonna's? Where's that?" I asked, thinking it was some insider place near the commission that was sponsored by the pop singer.

"You don' know Madonna's, man? Big Mac?" McDonald's. He was saying *McDonald's*.

"Hey, Linda, can you take this down for me?" Dr. Gonzalez interrupted, grabbing Tyrone's arm and applying a blood pressure cuff. "His pressure is ninety-nine over fifty-eight, and his pulse is—" he paused for several seconds, counting under his breath while reading his watch "—forty-eight. Lookin' good, dude."

"We just check pressure and pulses. Got it," I said, using the strategy of repeating what he had just said, as if I, too, had memorized the nonexistent guidebook.

"Yep, that's it. The inspectors do the rest. They weigh their gloves and check their wraps, too." I loved how easily he fed me information, desperate to show off what he knew. I was careful though, remembering not to ask *why* they weighed and checked. I figured I could corner an inspector before the end of the night to get those details.

We spent the next hour like that, Dr. Gonzalez checking in fighters and me filling out paperwork, checking pressures and pulses, and looking over last minute details. Through the curtains, I could hear the conference room filling up and was eager to see who was in the crowd.

As we were leaving, another man walked over. He was around five-foot-seven and stout, with tousled brown hair and large eyes. When our eyes met, he smiled, a smile so dangerously sincere, I almost let my guard down.

"Hey, Dr. Aziz! Thanks for showing up," Dr. Gonzalez said playfully, punching him in the shoulder.

"There're only four fights tonight, so I didn't think I needed to come in early. I had a ton of post-ops today, and my partner's out of town," Dr. Aziz said. His demeanor was confident but relaxed and, since he was talking about post-ops, he was obviously a surgeon. My guess was orthopedics. I couldn't imagine a neurosurgeon working the fights, but the irony of that would have been fantastic.

"You're the new recruit, right? Come with me, and we'll get set up by the ring." It took me a couple of seconds to realize he was addressing me. When I looked up and wordlessly pointed at myself, he smiled even more broadly, like he knew my secret.

In the conference room, the blue-carpeted floor was barely visible under the crowd of people. Men with long, buttoned overcoats spoke with exaggerated movements of their thick-ringed hands. Red-faced workmen laughed too hard and posed for pictures, fists holding plastic cups of alcohol. Along one wall stood a row of once-famous men and their overly perfumed girlfriends. To my surprise, of the few women I spotted, none were wearing ball gowns. When we reached the ring, we were stopped by a large man in a black suit, who held up his hand like a bridge troll, preventing our passing.

"Commission," Dr. Aziz said, holding up a gold badge with blue lettering. The security guard nodded and let us through. It looked like something a policeman would have, but he put it away too quickly for me to study it. I made a mental note that I needed to figure out how to get one of those things, whatever it was.

I followed Dr. Aziz to a long table on one side of the ring, where an older man was already seated, looking through some papers. He was wearing a light gray suit with very thin pinstripes and a pink tie. So close to the ring, he would be in for a surprise when the blood started flying. Apparently, he hadn't got the memo.

"Dr. Dahl, this is Dr. Williams, the chief medical examiner," Dr. Aziz said.

Dr. Williams glanced up and smirked. "Dr. Dahl. You trained at Manhattan Hospital, right?" His voice was deep and slow, like Barry White's younger brother. Dimples tugged at the insides of his cheeks under his mostly white beard. "That's where I trained. Great institution. Manhattan Hospital only trains the best. That's why I approved your application right away."

Finally, the mystery of how I had got there was solved. As desperate as I was to correct his mistake, I didn't dare, instead settling on, "I work there now." It wasn't a lie. I was just staying out of my own way. He didn't seem to care, continuing to smile and purse his lips.

The crowd's noise around us grew louder when the announcer entered the ring. "Good evening, ladies and gentlemen. Welcome to the Gerry Cooney Charity Fight for FIST. Cooney's fighting record of 28-3, including 24 knockouts, makes him one of the greatest fighters of all time! As you all know, he founded FIST, the Fighters' Initiative for Support and Training, to help retired boxers find jobs and transition into the next chapter of their lives. The organization also provides alcohol and drug counseling, job training, and educational and financial programs."

I was both impressed and saddened. It was great that

this guy, Cooney, made it out of the fight game on top, but the need for a charity to help broken-brained boxers was telling. Drug and alcohol counseling? It sounded more like a halfway house than a transitional program for former athletes. Retired basketball greats ended up with restaurant chains and sneaker endorsements. Worst-case scenario, they had enough neurons to work a desk job. These guys needed handouts to survive.

I looked around the crowd and vaguely recognized only one boxer. He was posing for photographs with fans, one hand in a fist, the other clutching a bottle of beer. Between shots, his aggressively cheery face relaxed into a blank stare, like he had an invisible on/off switch for the camera. Then it occurred to me—he was Roberto Duran. During the rematch with Sugar Ray Leonard, when he couldn't take the beating anymore, he was believed to have uttered those most infamous words that marred his legacy: *No más.* He seemed to be saying *no more* now, too.

The announcer continued. "In attendance tonight are boxing greats, Angelo Dundee, Jake LaMotta, and Ken Norton." When each name was announced, an old man with a cane stood up and waved to the audience. They looked frail and weathered. I couldn't imagine these guys crossing the street without assistance, let alone having gone at each other in the ring. No wonder they needed a charity.

"You know those guys, right?" Dr. Aziz asked, pulling the edge of his mouth into a half-smile. He knew I had no idea who they were, but he wasn't about to reveal my lie. He seemed to enjoy watching me squirm.

"Yes, of course, I mean, Jake LaMotta…" I said, pausing to let the silence speak for me. Then I remembered the announcer saying that Cooney had fought Ken Norton, so I continued. "And that fight with Cooney and Norton. I mean, c'mon!" I held out my hands, bouncing them up and down slowly in time with my head. He wasn't buying any of it.

The first fight of the night was the heavyweights. The announcers rambled statistics and titles, none of which meant anything to me. The fighters entered the ring with their entourages, who wore satin jackets and carried buckets, towels and bags. I barely recognized them from the night before, their faces made menacing by their mouthguards. After a few minutes, they gravitated to their respective corners and sat on stools. It felt like the best part of the night was about to begin.

I heard hooting and whistling from the audience and looked across the ring to the source of the attention: a woman dressed only in a bikini and fishnets. She was climbing the stairs, stabilized by the arm of a dreadlocked man. When she got to the platform, she lifted a card into the air and smiled. She walked around the ring, pausing at each corner to shift her weight from one hip to the other.

"What do you think of the ring girl?" Dr. Aziz asked, watching my expression change.

I thought a moment before answering. My initial reaction

was that I thought she was beautiful, all tight abs, perfect breasts and smooth skin. I had never in my life looked like that. And since I was conditioned, like every other young girl, to *want* to look that way, I was also jealous—too jealous to admit. I used to say that I was lucky I was born ugly. When I was younger, my crooked teeth and fat face forced me to find other parts of myself to use as assets. It was why I'd worked so hard in school and used self-awareness as a front for self-deprecation. But I couldn't admit any of that. I was supposed to look down on her for using her body instead of her brain. How else could I justify my life choices?

Before I could answer, the bell clanged, and the fighters were up. Their movements were measured and lazy, like they didn't want to waste energy until they got to the hitting part. I finally recognized one of the fighters as Juan. He looked terrifying, brows scrunched and eyes filled with something primal that made my heart beat faster. Sitting this close to the ring made everything more apparent. And transparent.

Juan moved in, ducking and swaying at his opponent's fetid punches. Even when he wasn't swinging, the other guy was on the defense. It was as if Juan's mere intention to hit was enough. After thirty seconds, the other fighter paused, breathless, and dropped his gloves for a fraction of a second. Then Juan went in for the kill, hitting the other boxer in the face, jaw and chest. Every blow landed hard, like a wet slap, sending an emulsion of bloody sweat into the air.

The liquid fell in thick drops, landing on the paper in

front of me, obscuring some of the words on the page. I stared at them, unable to move. I hadn't been in the presence of violent blood since residency. But now, instead of feeling disgusted, I was excited. I had never wanted to physically beat a man myself, but watching them hit each other felt cathartic. They were like living avatars for my own dark, internal video game.

Juan's opponent lost his footing, trying to walk backwards while his body moved in the opposite direction. He dropped to one knee and lowered his head, his upper body swaying from side to side, disconnected. Then the referee, who had been watching from a few feet away, walked over and stood in front of him, waving his arms and shaking his head that the fight was over.

I was rapt. Seeing the fight live and up close was nothing like watching it on television. The difference was like comparing tasting food made by a master chef to merely watching him prepare it through a glass screen. I almost felt like I'd knocked the guy out myself.

Dr. Aziz stood and grabbed me by the elbow, lifting me up from my seat. "We have to make sure he's okay. We have to go into the ring," he said, climbing onto his chair and stepping onto the table in front of us to reach the platform. Spreading the stretchy ropes wide, he climbed between them and held them open for me. I struggled, gracelessly contorting my body to fit through the narrow opening. I was glad I had taken Dr. Roy's advice about the shoes. It would have been impossible in heels.

Once inside the ring, I bristled, realizing my ineptitude now had a stage. I didn't know what to do with myself. If I stood and did nothing, my ignorance would be obvious. If I tried to help out, I would just get in the way. So I hovered behind, watching as Dr. Aziz helped the fighter to a stool and examined his eye movements. Dr. Aziz yelled questions I couldn't hear over the noise of the crowd. They sounded like the neuro exam from the night before, but simpler. The fighter was dazed but able to answer and still breathing heavily. As he swayed on the seat, officials stood behind him to prevent him from falling.

"We have to help him off, but first we have to see if he can do it himself. If we carry him off the stage, he'll lose his dignity. And that's even worse than losing the match," Dr. Aziz said, whispering close to my ear.

The fighter stood with the help of two men and wobbled a bit. Then he closed his eyes, took a deep breath and gathered his strength to walk across the platform and down the stairs. No one else seemed to notice his courage. The crowd was focused on the winner, cheering and clapping at his triumph.

Back at our seats, I could no longer hide the buzz of emotions that swept over me. I felt raw and alive. This violence didn't seem wrong. It seemed honest. It gave these men an outlet I didn't have—that very few in the professional world did. They got to express what the rest of us had to repress.

Dr. Aziz must have sensed my revelation. "Pretty cool, isn't it? I know we're here to patch them up and make sure they can fight, but our real job is to make sure they don't die. It's like we're doctors of war. Kind of anti-thetical to med school, huh?"

"Is it wrong to love the violence?" I asked, needing confirmation that I wasn't somehow breaking my Hip-pocratic Oath. I wasn't doing the actual harm, but I was condoning it, aiding and abetting like an accomplice.

"It's not wrong. You're just doing your job. Without us, it would just be barbaric. Sure, they have inspectors and judges, but we make it humane. New York is pretty strict, but other states let them get away with anything. Deaths still happen in boxing. Heck, there was a fight a couple of years ago on the *Intrepid*—" He stopped, real-izing he had already said too much.

"Whaddya think, Dr. Aziz?" the Chairman asked. He seemed to have come out of nowhere. "Is he gonna be okay?"

"Yeah, Fred is back there now checking on him. He was a little shaky though." They were talking about the loser, who was getting his final check in the locker room before being released home.

"This may be his last bout. He's been losing a lot lately, and each time he goes down a little quicker. I don't think I'll be able to let him keep fighting." The Chairman shook his head, saddened by his own words. He knew a lot about this fighter, and his concern seemed genuine. Maybe he really was the godfather of boxing but, in-stead of deciding who would die, he chose who to save.

"How's it going, Dr. Dahl? You learn something tonight?"

"Yes," I said, self-consciously. I had learned more about myself than boxing, but he didn't need to know that.

"So, it wasn't too much for you? The hitting? The blood?" he asked, ironic given my reaction.

"No, not too much at all. I loved it, actually. It reminded me of the Bronx, except back then I never got to see what happened to my patients to land them in the hospital." I smiled, trying to make light of the trauma.

"Listen, we know you're just figuring things out. Hell, I'm surprised you even applied for the position. I don't know any women who'd want to do this. We just needed to know you were tough enough to handle it," he said. I was both surprised and relieved. I had wasted the night trying to look smart, but all I really had to do was enjoy the violence.

"Oh, I'm tough enough to handle anything," I said, looking him straight in the eye. "I want to be here. This is where I belong."

7

"Let's go over some patients who may contact you over the weekend. I want to make sure they're well taken care of," Dr. Marsh said.

It was Friday afternoon, and we were sitting in the kitchen area of the office, reviewing the week's happenings. I was on call for the group, which meant I was covering patients usually seen by the other three doctors in addition to my own. This was not an easy feat. With 30,000 demanding, high-profile patients, I would be managing phone calls all weekend without access to their records. Dr. Marsh alone was expecting calls from one of the Kennedy clan, a major news reporter and a famous actor. I was looking forward to two and a half days of pure hell.

"Don't worry. They usually have their people call. They never do it themselves, so you'll have time to get a clear history," he said, making me feel more nervous than comforted. Although I wasn't impressed by people famous for the sake of fame, everyone in the office made such a fuss over them it stressed me out.

I had asked Dr. Marsh once how he dealt with it, and he'd explained, "That depends on what you consider famous. I once treated a musician I really admired. No one else knew who he was, but to me he was so impressive, I was a little nervous. But he was cool. We ended up having a lot in common and later became pretty good friends. I still see him whenever he's in town."

He was right. What was fame, really? In the most basic sense, it was familiarity: recognizing someone who didn't recognize you back. And since I didn't know who most of these people were, it didn't matter as much to me.

On my way home, minutes after stepping out of the office, my pager went off. I cringed. Sensitized by five years of residency, the beeping was like an invisible, electric dog collar. Every time it went off, I was stunned into stopping whatever I was doing and submitting to its high-pitched whine. Nothing that was happening in my life trumped its urgency. Not eating. Or using the toilet. Or sex. Once, in my third year, I'd had to hang up on my crying husband, who had just lost his mentor, because the recovery room needed me. All these years later, I still had mini panic attacks every time it went off.

Pulse escalating, I glanced at the screen to make sure it wasn't one of Dr. Marsh's important ones.

Patient call. Ear pain. Please call back.

A pit of dread collected in my stomach. I needed to calm myself, so I ignored the page for the time it took me to get home. Ear pain was not an emergency, so a few minutes wouldn't make a difference. When I reached the lobby of my apartment, the pager went off again.

Patient call. Ear pain SEVERE. Please call.

This patient was relentless. But weren't they all? Couldn't it wait five minutes? Suffocating a scream, I took a deep breath and dialed the number.

"Hello, this is Dr. Dahl. I'm on call for the weekend. How can I help you?" I asked, my mouth automatically forming the words while my brain replayed Juan's magnificent knockout punch.

"Hello, is this the doctor?" a man's voice said on the other line. I was shocked. It was the effeminate and undeniable voice of my favorite fashion designer. I went silent.

When I had been accepted to medical school, I was in my senior year of college at the University of Minnesota. Because I was responsible for my own tuition, I worked two to three student jobs at a time to make ends meet. In the name of efficiency, these jobs, which ranged from administering heroin and cocaine to lab rats, to squashing fruit flies for their DNA, had doubled as résumé builders. Once I had reached my goal of getting into med school, I'd decided to indulge in a job that didn't entail killing or maiming. As luck would have it, there had been an opening in the costume department of the theater—a job that would inspire a whole new side of me.

Weeks in, I was already questioning my career choice. Hours of pinning, cutting and sewing flew by like minutes as we sculpted three-dimensional pieces of art from flat pieces of fabric, art that danced around the stage on the bodies of actors. I'd been smitten. I wanted to spend the rest of my life making clothing. I couldn't see myself doing anything else.

After graduation, I had given up my acceptance to medical school and went to work in a costume shop. But it was a far cry from my college job. Countless hours in a windowless warehouse gave me plenty of time to consider my end game. My father's voice grew louder in my head. With each bleeding finger, he reminded me I was no one without money. No matter how creative I thought I was, no one else cared. The world was full of starving artists betraying their art with side jobs. If I wanted to be anybody, I had to go to medical school. So that's what I did.

But my dream hadn't died there. I'd clung to it like the *Vogue* magazines I carried on hospitals rounds, inspecting the anatomy of dresses as meticulously as I did bodies, and studying prêt-à-porter collections so I could copy them with my sewing machine. I memorized the name of each model, deluded that the clothes draped on their emaciated frames would look the same on my stout one. Of all the designers I had worshipped, there had been two who had impacted me the most. One was now dead. The other was on the phone with me at this very moment. I felt like the Beatles' biggest groupie being summoned by John Lennon.

Forgetting myself, I dissolved into starstruck madness. "Is this really you? Oh my God. I *love* you! I mean, wow, am I really talking to you? You're the reason I got through med school..." Compliments poured from my mouth like waste from an ostomy. I gushed over his designs: "Understated, yet sophisticated." I blathered about his "genius, utter genius!" of incorporating a box pleat into a high-waisted pant. I told him how I used to sew clothes from fabric scraps to look like his because I couldn't afford the "good stuff." I even talked about how I would visit the Fashion Institute of Technology on rare days off during residency, dreaming of one day attending classes. When I finally paused, there was quiet on the other end.

"I trained at Parson's. I can't tell you anything about FIT," he said, more than a little annoyed. Parson's School of Design was high-end. It was like comparing Harvard to a state school. "Can I tell you about my ear now?"

"Yes, uh, sorry. I'm all ears. Get it? Ears?" I joked, struggling to make light of my blunder. But he didn't laugh. I simultaneously wanted to pass out and to puke.

As he spoke, I tried hard to focus on his complaints. I heard words like *pain* and *ear* and *smelly discharge*, but my mind was elsewhere. I was thinking that, if I helped him, he would be so grateful he would grow to like me, like Dr. Marsh's musician patient. He may even invite me to visit his studio so I could see what I had missed by becoming a doctor. We could become friends. The possibilities were endless.

There was another pause on the phone. "Hello, Dr. Dahl? Are you there?"

"Yes," I said. I couldn't believe he had just said my name. "It sounds like you have an ear infection. Let me call in some drops, and you can come in and see me in the office on Monday." My heart was pounding. As the words left my mouth, I realized there was a very good chance that once he met me in person, he would forgive me. There was still hope for our friendship.

"Okay. Here is my pharmacy number. Thanks," he said, spitting the number into the phone before hanging up.

The abrupt click of the receiver triggered a litany of shame. I had completely screwed up. Instead of acting cool, I had been needy like a groupie. Barely registering his symptoms, I had probably misdiagnosed him. Or worse—I had diagnosed him too quickly. I had told him to come to the office Monday, but what if he was better by then and didn't need me? I had just spoken to the one person I had wanted to meet more than anyone, and he probably hated me.

Just before Thanksgiving, the other doctors were away, so my schedule was, once again, bombarded by their overflow. More seasoned by time, I had become adept at handling their patients' exhausting expectations. One strategy I utilized was answering their questions with more questions. If they were skeptical about my experience and asked how many procedures I had done, I would laugh, batting back, "You mean this year?" Another strategy was sarcasm. When accused of being too young to know what I was talking about, I would steal a phrase from my boxing friends. "I may look young, but I'm wrinkled on the inside." False confidence was another gem. "When I operate, everyone in the room stops to observe," I would say. "I settle for no less than perfection." I got so used to fielding criticism, I treated every patient encounter like a game of tennis. And, so far, I was ahead a few points.

"I have the worst ear pain. When the plane landed it was the most excruciating thing I've ever felt. Also, I can't hear, and there is this terrible ringing." The man seated in the exam chair was impeccably dressed. He wore a pressed white shirt, wool pants and a cashmere sweater tied around his shoulders. His blond hair, peppered with silver and gray, topped a cleanly shaven face that could have been the focal point of a Ralph Lauren ad.

Dressed in my usual boxy Ann Taylor suit, I felt self-conscious. I appreciated the brand because it catered to *mature* women with inflated sizing. In Ann's world, I was a perfect size six with a waistband that didn't cut off the circulation to my lower body. But my outfit was far from sophisticated. Next to this patient, I looked like an amateur.

"Where were you flying from?" I asked, forgetting myself. It didn't really matter, but I loved hearing about these people—how they spent vacations, who they knew, what they did for work. It made the windows of my prison more transparent. Even if I couldn't live their lives, I could at least imagine them.

"Well, I started off in London. Then I flew to Switzerland, and we went skiing at St. Moritz. Have you ever been there? The next time you go, I'll tell you where to dine." I had never been to St. Moritz, but not only because I'd never been to Switzerland: I had also never been skiing and wouldn't have had a clue how to act or dress on the slopes. But I nodded anyway, playing the game the only way I knew how.

"So you flew, and then went skiing. Did you have a cold?" I was relatively certain he had an ear infection. But because it rarely happened in adults, there had to be extenuating circumstances, like stuffy sinuses, coupled with extreme changes in barometric pressure.

"Yes I did! How did you know?" he asked, surprised and almost giddy. "I'm impressed that someone so young and new in practice would know something like that," he said, inadvertently turning his compliment into an insult.

I reeled internally, then proceeded with the exam. I would have to prove myself another way.

I peered into his ear, at one of the worst middle-ear infections I had ever seen. His drum was thick and red and oozing with pus. Although it wasn't cancer, the diagnostic term for his condition underscored its seriousness: malignant otitis media. Without immediate intervention, he could permanently lose his hearing, but I didn't want to alarm him. I kept my statements simple and calm. "I'm gonna have to drain your ear," I said. "It's really infected."

"What do you mean drain it? Like with a suction?" he asked, smiling like I had just told him he was getting candy. His responses were so odd, I couldn't tell if he was confused or delirious from pain medication.

"Not exactly. I'll have to numb your eardrum and then puncture it to drain the fluid." I expected him to refuse or at least show some fear, but he just nodded, like a little boy accepting directions from his teacher.

"I trust you," he said. His words were powerful, filling my tragic ego with real confidence.

I forged on without words, numbing his eardrum with topical lidocaine, then magnifying it with a microscope. Using a tiny scalpel, I pierced the drum, releasing thick, yellow pus through the hole, and draining it with a metal ear suction. Once cleared, I placed a plastic, bobbin-shaped tube into the hole and dripped antibiotics into his middle ear. Altogether, it took less than ten minutes.

"Wow, I feel better already!" he said, as I was returning his chair to the upright position. "I have to say, you are just spectacular. I am just so, so impressed." His enthusiasm was so robust, I thought he was mocking me. People like him usually made me work hard to earn their respect. He was actually being nice.

"Let me ask you something. Do you think you would be free for lunch sometime this week? I really want to thank you, and I know this great little Italian place around the corner."

I couldn't believe my ears. Did this successful, wealthy man want to be my friend because of the way I took care of him? This must be how my colleagues connected with important people, like chairmen and presidents of things. All my hard work and fending off pretentious attitudes were finally paying off. I had to say yes.

"I would be happy to. Just give me a date, and I will make it work," I said casually, like it happened all the time. I wasn't about to repeat the mistake I had made with the designer and get too excited, but going out for lunch was tricky. My overbooked schedule didn't allow for breaks. I barely had time to shove food in my mouth between patients. But, for this special occasion, I would make it happen. We planned a date for later that week.

"Are you feeling better?" I asked, sitting across from him at the restaurant. He had arrived before me and was already sipping on a glass of wine.

"So much better. I can finally hear, and I don't even need the pain meds anymore. Can I order a glass for you?" he asked, pointing at his. His face was flushed, which made me wonder if he had a wine allergy. But I reminded myself I was not a doctor today, I was a person. I was not allowed to diagnose.

As a person, I wanted nothing more than to down some Pinot Grigio to calm my nerves, but I had to refuse. I still had to go back and see my afternoon patients. "No, I'll just have some ice tea, thanks."

"So, Dr. Dahl, are you married? I didn't notice a ring." He shifted a little in his chair and flung his fingers toward my hands. It was a strange gesture, but I figured he was just trying to get to know me.

"No, not anymore," I said, before I could stop myself. I didn't want him to judge me for my failed marriage, so I added, "I married my first boyfriend," as a buffer. It also gave me an excuse for when he would undoubtedly ask what my ex-husband did for a living. I was surprised when he didn't.

"Ah, you're lucky. Marriage isn't easy. I've been married a long time—too long. Jane is great but, after a while, people just drift apart." He looked sad. I appreciated that he was sharing this part of himself.

"I know what you mean. I used to love spending time with my husband. But, as time went on, we just wanted different things." It felt good to be able to speak openly. I was so tired of holding in all those feelings; it was a relief to have a real conversation about it.

We continued, explaining how we had met our prospective spouses: both in college. He told me about his children (he had three), his hobbies (yoga and, of course, skiing), where he'd grown up (Vermont). Talking to him felt so good it made me realize how lonely I had become.

"You seem to really get me," he said, leaning in and touching my hand. "I don't usually connect with people this way, not this quickly. I feel like I could tell you anything."

I froze. Had this friendship talk suddenly turned into something else? Was I reading into it or walking backwards into a land mine? I was being delusional. He couldn't be hitting on me. He was married and spent most of the lunch talking about his family. He was obviously just being nice. How could someone like him want someone like me? I was nothing like his wife.

I glanced at his watch, resting so near my wrist: it was time to get back to the office. I thanked him for lunch and left, laughing at myself for thinking such crazy thoughts.

When he called the office the following week with the proposal that I become his mistress, I blamed myself.

"She will never divorce me—well, we will never divorce each other. We have to stay together for the kids. But we haven't been together for some time, if you know what I mean," he said, explaining his situation in practical terms. Despite my horror at his request, I respected his honesty. He had clearly thought this through.

"That is a predicament," I said. I had never been in a situation like this, and I didn't know what to do. He was still my patient, and I didn't want to get in trouble with my bosses, so I tried to doctor him through his harassment of me.

"Well, that's where you come in. Even though my wife wants to stay married, there are parts she no longer wants. Parts I could share with you…"

I couldn't believe my ears. Why would he think I would want to be with a married man? Didn't I deserve better than someone who would hide me, or be ashamed to be seen with me? And what about his poor wife?

"Oh, uh, wow. That's, wow. That's something. I'm sorry, but no. You are my patient and, as your doctor, it's really inappropriate," I said, more furious that I was hiding behind my profession instead of telling him what I really thought of his proposition. My true sentiments would have definitely gotten me fired.

"Well, if you reconsider, you know where to find me," he said before hanging up, unfazed and still hopeful.

I thought that would be the last I heard from him, but it wasn't. He still made appointments and, because I was too embarrassed to explain to my colleagues what had happened, I kept seeing him. With each visit, I navigated around his impudence like it was my fault. I figured I was to blame for the supposed misunderstanding because I'd had lunch with him.

I wish I could say he was the only wealthy married man who propositioned me, but the Upper East Side had an epidemic. There was the hedge-fund manager who asked me to be his girlfriend, even though his wife was also my patient, then fired me when I refused. And the real-estate mogul who wanted me to be his lover, when his wife and other girlfriend were away, but first I had to refill his Viagra prescription. There was the plastic surgeon whose personal space shrank to fractions of an inch when he saw me, whispering patient referrals into my ear with hot breath. And the octogenarian diplomat who tried to caress my behind with his bony fingers, while I was checking his throat. It seemed like the more money these men accumulated, the less need they had for decency. Everything was a commodity, including me. The irony was that, after spending most of my life as an untouchable, I finally had more male attention than I could handle. But it was the kind that disgusted me. I would have given anything to go back to being invisible.

"Have you always been in private practice?" I asked Dr. Marsh one day. He had invited me into his office, as he often did, to listen to a new song he liked.

"No. I worked for the hospital right out of fellowship. It was a great way to start out because of the internal referral system," he said.

"So, why did you leave?"

"You want to know the truth? I loved working there, but the department chair made the call schedule a living hell. The workload was ridiculous for what they were paying me." He sighed, scrolling through his playlist. "Did you ever consider working for a hospital?"

"Not really. The job security is nice, but I'm terrible at politics. I don't think anyone in my residency program was sad to see me go," I said, referring to my exceedingly short temper when it came to bureaucracy.

"You just have to learn how to play the game, that's all. Listen to this." A slow song with twangy guitar and moody vocals drizzled out of his computer. "The chair is retiring. Have you heard? I wonder how they'll handle that."

"Would you ever consider going back?" I asked.

"To the hospital? Never. That would be like selling my soul to the devil." He closed his eyes and swung his head from side to side, lost in the song.

I wanted so badly to tell him about the boxing thing, but I kept it to myself. It was my dirty little secret and so at odds with the image he had painstakingly created for the practice that I knew he would fire me if he ever found out. But even at the risk of losing my day job, I wouldn't give up boxing. The rebel in me loved the potential of his discovering it almost as much as the obedient student feared it. But there was no way he would find out. No one ever noticed the fight doctors.

"I want to introduce you to some people," the Chairman said, greeting me as I walked through the door of the Hammerstein Ballroom.

He had given me my second fight assignment in close succession to the first, which was a good sign. When I got there, the venue was still empty, and the crews were setting up the ring. He led me past the empty seats to a group of men standing near the entrance to the backstage area.

"This must be the famous Dr. Dahl," one of the men said. He was young, with a scruffy beard that outlined his pleasant face. He wore a brown suit and a shirt that was unbuttoned at the top.

"Why am I famous?" I asked, assuming he meant *in-famous*. The Chairman had probably been sharing stories about how hard I was trying not to look stupid at the last fight.

"We hear you're a very successful doctor in Manhattan," said another, older man. He said the middle *a* in *Manhattan* with such a wide open mouth his tongue didn't come forward enough to enunciate the *ts*. He wore a black turtleneck made of tightly knit merino wool and black pants that were held up with a thin belt. He was shorter than the other men. "I'm Sal, by the way. I run some things. And this, over here, is Seth." He gestured to the younger man. "His family owns *Everlast*. You know 'em? The boxing-gear company." Of course I had heard of *Everlast*. Their logo was everywhere, even on the gloves.

"The practice I work for is really great, but I'm not a partner or anything," I said, confessing my status. I had no idea why they thought so highly of me. Even though I had been through a lot, every advancement had the paradoxical effect of making me feel more worthless.

"You are too humble, Dr. Dahl. You've accomplished so much at such a young age." It was the Chairman now. How could these men, who were obviously successful and connected, have such high regard for me? Due to my history, I was cautious in accepting their compliments. I didn't want the extra burden of having to meet expectations that simply weren't true.

"Well, you're the first woman I've met who has the

balls—uh, excuse me—the guts to be a fight doctor. You should be proud of yourself," Sal said. His words made me realize that, of all the emotions I had felt, pride was one of the more elusive ones. But here I was, surrounded by men who were finally showing me some respect. I couldn't help but accept it.

Our conversation was interrupted by one of the officials. He leaned into the Chairman, whispering something about gloves.

"Let's go, Dr. Dahl. We have to check something out in the back with one of the managers. Gentlemen," he said, nodding to the men to bid them leave. They nodded back in wordless understanding.

The Chairman was silent until we reached one of the dressing rooms. Through the open door, I saw an inspector holding a pair of red boxing gloves and speaking to another man in Spanish. I didn't understand their words, but their flailing fingers and exasperated expressions seemed to indicate some kind of disagreement.

"*¿Cómo estás?*" the Chairman asked after him. Even he knew Spanish. I knew only a few medical phrases, but *saca la lengua* wasn't so useful in everyday conversation, when you weren't asking someone to stick out their tongue.

"I try to 'splain, *los* gloves, they are *siempre* the same as *ultima* fight." The manager was speaking his best Spanglish, that mix of Spanish and English that spawned words like *jamberger* and made any English word sound Spanish by putting an *el* or *los* in front of it. He continued his argument, explaining that "*el* parking *esta* berry bad" and "no *hay tiempo* to change *los* gloves."

"Miguel, we have limits on how much the gloves are allowed to weigh in New York state. I know these gloves were fine at the last fight, but that's because it was in Puerto Rico." The Chairman spoke very loudly, articulating each word with the assumption that Miguel would better understand him with more volume. But, judging by Miguel's focused eyes, it was clear that, although he was trying very hard, he had no idea what the Chairman was saying.

The inspector, taking his rightful place in the conversation, let out a flurry of rolled *r*s and sharp *s*s that made the Chairman's point clear in real Spanish. Miguel threw up his hands and turned his head to the side in defeat.

"Well, that's one less fight for tonight," the Chairman said. "Linda, you know why we weigh the gloves, right? Because sometimes they put pieces of metal or other objects in there that can really hurt the other guy." He was so calm in his delivery, it was like he was Yoda to my Luke Skywalker. We walked down the stairs back to the main area, almost bumping into Dr. Gonzalez.

"Hey, guys, anyone back there?" He seemed to have just arrived, which was confusing because the Chairman had told me to come thirty minutes earlier.

"Yeah, there are some fighters in the back. Victor's manager brought the wrong gloves. Joey's trying to get him another pair, but it looks like the fight's gonna be cancelled. You can take Dr. Dahl with you," he said, turning abruptly and leaving.

"Hey, you know who's downstairs?" Dr. Gonzalez asked, excitedly. "That guy whose family owns Everlast. I've been trying to talk to him for years, and I finally met him at the last fight. Hopefully he'll remember me tonight. And that dude with him, Sal. He's a big deal. His company sponsors all the fights in the city." He was talking about the men I had met downstairs.

For some reason, the Chairman was taking me under his wing. Finally, a powerful man wasn't trying to sleep with me. He was making me his protégée.

Although my gender didn't go unheeded, I continued to be impressed by the way men treated me in the world of boxing. It was old-school male behavior, something I was groomed to reject. But, after being treated like a notch on the proverbial bedpost of the Upper East Side, I now appreciated the chivalry. Doors were held open, men stepped aside as I passed and I was rarely called by my first name. Being a female fight doctor meant I was both revered and protected. I got all the benefits of being the so-called weaker sex without any of the oppression.

Between rounds, when I had to go into the ring to check a fighter, I was taken by the hand and helped up the stairs. If a fighter was bleeding, the corner men moved out of the way, saying "*Mira, mira, mami*. Look the cuts," which was in distinct contrast to my male counterparts, who were barely allowed a glimpse.

As Frank once explained, "Usually, when the doctor goes up there, the cut men won't let him in to get a look.

They cover up the boxer so the doctor won't disqualify him. With you, it's like carte blanche. They practically give you a welcome party!"

The cut men even gave me pointers and showed me tricks of their trade. At one fight, a boxer got knocked in the face so hard, he had a split brow and bloody nose. With only sixty seconds to stop the bleeding, his team descended on him. I watched as his cut man pulled out the largest rectal swab I had ever seen and shoved it up the boxer's nose, compressing his nostrils against it. I cringed, horrified but impressed at his using something meant for a much larger hole to control bleeding in such a small one.

Leaving the swab in place, he then dipped a piece of gauze in clear liquid and pressed it above the boxer's brow with such pressure the boxer had to forcefully push back to prevent whiplash. Within seconds, the bleeding stopped.

I leaned in to examine the clean, and now dry, laceration. "What was that liquid?" I asked, amazed, and certain he would lie and tell me it was saline.

"Epinephrine," he whispered. "Don't tell no one. We're not supposed to use it. I'm training to be a scrub nurse, so I get from the hospital."

"What about the swab? How did you figure that out?" I asked, pointing at the wooden stick that still extended from the boxer's nostril.

"Oh," he laughed. "The secret is Vaseline."

I got to meet boxing greats, who stopped everything to take pictures with the Lady Fight Doctor. I met George

Foreman and Lennox Lewis when they were announcing. Bernard Hopkins posed for a picture with me before ducking away from other fans. I was even invited to a private dinner with Sultan Ibragimov, whose father warned me not to "squeeze the Charmin" as we posed for a picture. For the first time, being a woman made my job easier instead of harder.

"Everyone is so nice. I can't believe I am getting trained so quickly. And the Chairman is so supportive," I told Dr. Roy one day. I felt so happy. I was finally getting the respect I deserved, and I wasn't taking any of it for granted.

"Yes, about that—" He stopped himself midthought and considered before continuing. "You know what? I'm just gonna let you see for yourself. And I'll leave it at that." His cryptic warning left me feeling uneasy, but I didn't want to press him. I wanted this fantasy to last as long as possible. And if his warning was going to break the spell, I didn't want to know.

"He's on my schedule? How did that happen? Do you know who he is?" I asked the secretary. She shrugged and twisted a curl of orange hair between her fingers.

"I don't know. Some designer dude?" She pursed her lips together and lifted her full upper lip so high it almost touched the edge of her nostrils. She was so bored with my excitement I didn't bother to explain.

It had been months since that ill-fated phone call, and I had given up on ever seeing him again. But now that my self-esteem was inching higher because of boxing, I was hopeful. This could be my chance to recover what I had originally messed up. I collected myself, remembering Lennox and George, and walked into the room.

"Hi! I'm Dr. Dahl. So nice to finally meet you in person," I said. To my surprise and sadness, the man sitting on the exam chair bore little resemblance to the one I remembered from the pages of glossy magazines.

Swirled into an unkempt mess, hair sprang from his head like he had just crawled out of bed. His graying beard cast a gloom over sagging cheeks. He wore a sour look and pants that could only be referred to as *highwaters*, fully exposing his lace-up shoes and lack of socks. Although he shared similar characteristics with the man I had admired, this person could not possibly be him. I could barely hide my disappointment.

"Oh God, it's you," he said, extending the word *you* into a near whine and rolling his eyes when he saw me. "They said Dr. Marsh was out, but I didn't realize you were the only one left."

I hadn't realized I had made such a strong impression. Seeing there was little I could do to salvage the relationship, personal or professional, I decided to just attend to him and get it over with. I had treated dignitaries and rock stars in residency because it was my duty. How hard would it be to treat an angry diva.

"What's going on with your ear? Is it still hurting?"

"I was kind of skeptical when you prescribed the drops. They worked at first, but then they stopped. Dr. Marsh usually gives me different ones, but you got so worked up on the phone I couldn't think straight and forgot to tell you." He stuck his index finger into his left ear and twisted it back and forth. When he pulled out the tip, it was coated with a sticky substance that had the faint odor of sulfur.

Concealing my revulsion, I peered into his ear. Thick white mucous coated his irritated canal like milk pudding. His eardrum was covered in tiny red bumps, which meant he had tried to relieve the itching by scratching it with a foreign object. "What did you put in your ear? Did you use Q-tips?"

"Well, it itches like hell. What do you expect me to do? It's driving me crazy! I used Q-tips, bobby pins, pens and whatever else would fit in there." He was getting more upset and defensive with each question, as if I were to blame for his infection.

"It looks like you still have an external otitis—I mean swimmer's ear. Did you keep your ear dry?" I was trying not to talk down to him, but the medical words came out faster than the lay ones.

"You didn't *tell* me to keep my ear dry." He was right. In my frenzy over his phone call, I had forgotten to give him that instruction. Usually the drops worked, but if his ear had been subject to additional water, I wasn't surprised it was still infected.

"It looks like the dampness and Q-tips prevented the infection from healing. Now you are growing fungus. It's like athlete's foot in your ear." That was an awful comparison, but it was true.

"In my ear? That's disgusting!"

"It happens—"

"Oh my God, what do I do? I can't live like this, with this itching and the smell..." He was nearing the point of hysteria, when I realized the real problem. He was scared because he didn't trust me.

I sat back down on my stool so I could look him straight in the eye. "This infection is very treatable," I said. "It may take some time, but we can get rid of it."

"How in the hell are we going to do that!?" he nearly yelled, snapping out the words with liquid spittle that landed on my face. He hated me, but I had to keep going. If I let his anxiety get the better of me, I would fail him. I could live with his never wanting to be my friend, but I couldn't live with being an inadequate doctor.

"I will prescribe a different medication for you. The drops may burn a little at first, but you have to use them so you get better. And you have to keep your ears completely dry. If you must use Q-tips, put some cortisone on them first so it calms down the itching." He quieted and continued listening, finally looking me in the eye.

"Next week, you can come back and see Dr. Marsh so he can make sure everything has healed." I knew he never wanted to see me again, and I wanted him to see that I understood that.

When he finally left, he was less agitated but hardly serene, clutching my prescription in his hand like divorce papers. At that moment I took hold of my ego, blindfolded and silenced her, and put her in the corner.

8

Every breed of doctor has a national organization. My own specialty has the American Academy of Otolaryngology, whose yearly meetings alternate between the East and West Coasts and draw in many of the country's over 9,000 practicing ENTs. I shouldn't have been surprised to learn that fight doctors have their own group: the American Association of Professional Ringside Physicians, or AAPRP for short. They also have an annual meeting. When I had first heard about it, I laughed. Not only because I confused it with the similar sounding association for retired persons, the AARP. I also couldn't see how the unofficial, hands-on New York style of fight doctoring could translate into a lecture format. For all I knew, we would be trapped in an over-air-conditioned conference room for two days, talking about boxing stats and trading Outback Steakhouse coupons.

The conference was held in Las Vegas, the boxing epicenter of the country. I had been there only once, a few years prior, when my conservative older sister had invited me. After perusing indoor shopping malls and sunning by the pool, she had insisted we retire to our prospective beds by 8:00 p.m. The very sins she wanted to avoid were the only reasons anyone visited the city in the first place. More than a small part of me hoped this trip would make up for my last train wreck.

The conference room the AAPRP had reserved at the Luxor Hotel was tiny, with only five or six round tables, a small projection screen and no refreshments. Taking a chair next to Dr. Gonzalez, I berated myself for not stopping at the Starbucks kiosk on the way in. Even with coffee, staying awake would present a challenge. I counted a total of twenty people at the tables. The only other woman was the conference assistant, who was checking everyone in.

"Did you get any rest on the plane?" Dr. Landau asked, joining us at the table. He was in his mid- to late-fifties, with chin-length gray hair that he tucked behind his ears and a drawn-out New York accent.

"I always sleep on planes. It's a gift, really," I said. Sleep was one thing that never escaped me, but it wasn't always a gift. I remembered a middle-of-the-night laparoscopic bowel case in residency when I had fallen asleep. It wouldn't have been so bad if I hadn't been standing up, holding the camera. But even the bumpy ride the surgeons endured from my narcoleptic bobs hadn't been enough to excuse me from the case.

"That schmuck from Ohio's here. Who the hell boxes

in Ohio?" Dr. Landau asked, looking around the room at the empty tables. I had no idea who he was referring to.

"Don't they box in all the states?" I asked. I assumed that this national organization represented the whole country. It hadn't occurred to me that some states didn't have boxing. Places like North Dakota could have used it. There was plenty of time to train, especially when wheat surpluses meant farmers were paid by the government *not* to farm. And the men were burly enough. I used to call them *corn-fed*.

"No, only in twenty-odd states. New York, New Jersey and Nevada are the big ones, but there's also Connecticut because of the casinos. The rest of them—agh—I don't know why they even bother," he said, pushing his glasses up to meet his face. "You're probably the only ENT, did you know that?"

"Really?" I asked. I was so conscious of being the only female ringside doctor in New York, it hadn't occurred to me that I was another kind of only. "What other types of doctors are there?"

"Lots: orthopedics, rehab, family practice, internists," Dr. Gonzalez piped in.

"There's even a psychiatrist," Dr. Landau said.

"How does that work? If a fighter gets knocked out, does he run into the ring and ask about his childhood?" I realized as soon as I had said it that it was probably a fitting approach.

"There's also a radiologist. What do you think of that? Personally, I don't think it really matters. If you're a doctor, it means you've made it through med school and you're smart, and if you're willing to work for the peanuts they pay us, you're obviously a huge boxing fan. You'll make sure no one gets hurt," he said.

He had a point. For a whole night's work, the doctors were paid less than a single patient visit in the office. I disagreed with the rest of his argument, but I didn't dare say it out loud. Getting into medical school didn't automatically translate into genius. Not all doctors are created equal, nor does their purported intelligence mean they have common sense. There is a running joke that goes: *Do you know what they call the person who graduates last in their medical school class? Answer: Doctor.* I had already heard of one death in New York on a ship, called the *Intrepid*, and many others injuries, fatal and otherwise, in Las Vegas. And although I didn't know the rules of boxing, thanks to the Bronx I knew more about head trauma than I ever wanted to know. With all the other injuries boxers sustained, head trauma was the one that could kill them, yet very few of these specialists were trained in that.

We sat through the first lecture about the history of the AAPRP by its founder, Dr. Michael Schwartz, the chief medical examiner of the Connecticut Athletic Commission. Still a young organization, the AAPRP had only been around since 1997, hence the sparse membership and lack of free coffee. It turned out that every state operated its commission with their own set of rules. Dr. Schwartz's main goal was to establish bare-minimum medical standards for boxers that would be adopted by commissions of every state. Although the federal Professional Boxing Safety Act had been passed in 1996, there was no national governing body to enforce it. I was surprised to learn that most states didn't even do basic evaluations, like eye exams and MRIs. And the regulations differed so much from state to state that promoters used that disparity to their advantage, holding risky fights in states with lenient rules. Apparently, New York was known as having the toughest commission of all. And here I was, thinking it was lax.

More lectures followed: lectures on hand trauma, head trauma, eye trauma. A former boxer talked about his relationship with the commission. He explained that boxers didn't see the doctors as protectors. They saw us as enforcers. They often lied about injuries so we wouldn't pull them out of fights for medical reasons. For the boxers, the goal wasn't safety. The goal was to stay in the ring. At any cost.

The memory center of my head was spinning, searching for a place to store all I didn't know, when I noticed a woman standing near the podium. Tall and lanky, she had a shock of unnaturally red hair that lay limp on her shoulders. It was the great Dr. Margaret Goodman. She was the only other female fight doctor I had ever heard of and, although women were usually marginalized in medicine, she was, ironically, the most famous fight doctor in Nevada. If there was ever a role model for me in this sport, it was her. She had worked some of the biggest fights in recent history, and there she stood, at the front of the room. We were on a break between lectures, so all I had to do was go up and talk to her. I couldn't pass up the opportunity.

"Hi, Dr. Goodman. I'm Linda Dahl. I'm a doctor in New York," I said, extending my hand, nervously.

She looked up, briefly making eye contact, and offered a reluctant handshake. When she looked away without speaking, I tried again, assuming she hadn't heard me. Maybe I was too vague.

"I'm a fight doctor in New York," I repeated. "I really admire your work. You're so well respected—" I stopped speaking when she turned to engage the man next to her in conversation. It was like I was invisible. Stunned and embarrassed, I couldn't understand why she wouldn't talk to me. Maybe she was shy. Or perhaps I expected too much.

During residency, when I had been rotating through a hospital in Long Island, Hillary Clinton had paid a visit to a neighboring hospital. She and Bill had occupied the White House during my entire medical training, and I was a huge fan. She was such a strong woman, the way she held her own with her philandering husband and ran for Senate while he was finishing his term in office. So, when I had heard she was speaking, I bartered, negotiated and lied to get away long enough to hear her. I wanted to bathe in her presence.

Still in scrubs and praying I wouldn't get caught, I arrived just in time. The event was held under an outdoor tent on the hospital lawn, and I found a chair in the back row. I felt so proud to be there—rooted like the legs of my chair, which were sinking into the damp grass under my weight.

Hillary stood at the front of the room in a cornflower-blue suit, hair perfectly coiffed and helmet-shaped. Although she looked the part of a political wife, she operated like a senator. Every statement, every comment was immaculately crafted. She referenced personal comments from the crowd and earlier speakers, seamlessly weaving them into her responses. She was a genius negotiator and powerful figure in Congress. I was infatuated.

After the speech, standing in line behind other hospital workers, I prepared my five-second blurb. I couldn't believe I had the chance to meet her, and I wanted her to see how important she was to me and other female surgeons. We were invading fields of men like she was.

I approached the table, ready with words strung into sentences. "I am so happy to meet you, Senator Clinton. I'm a surgical resident at the hospital, and I wanted you to know how much I admire you. There are so few women in the program, and you're such an inspiration to all of us." I was so nervous, my eyes darted around the tent as I spoke, looking up when I said the words *admire* and *inspiration*. When I finished, I finally met her gaze, excited to see her reaction. But instead of the raised eyebrows and prideful smirk I was expecting, her expression was cold and empty. Her tight lips wouldn't even part for a fake smile. She was so bored she may as well have been listening to her housekeeper talk about laundry detergent.

In that instant, I had lost my crush on her. It's true that public figures don't always live up to our individual needs, but this seemed basic. And not unusual when it came to women in male-heavy environments. When we reach more powerful positions, women rarely champion other women. In my own specialty, women didn't band together to support each other. In fact, we did the opposite, getting out of the line of fire, or aligning ourselves with supportive men instead.

There was one woman in my program who was sick of the sexist comments and offensive requests that we all faced every day. But, unlike the rest of us, she'd chosen to fight back. When one attending nuzzled his nose into her neck during a case, she called him a creep and shoved him off. When another intertwined stories of his philandering with surgical instruction, she refused to listen and scrubbed out of the case. But there were consequences to her actions. The men labeled her a troublemaker and blackballed her in all the hospitals. Even after graduation, every time she applied for privileges, she had to send a letter of recommendation from the department chair. But it was never a real recommendation. It was no surprise that she ended up in a small-town hospital in New Jersey.

But the rest of us had done nothing to support her. We were all out for ourselves. When a powerful surgeon told me to *Come and sit on Papa's lap* if I wanted to perform the surgeries, I had obliged. When another told me to make sure my husband knew not to get me pregnant during residency, I had laughed it off and agreed. Other women used different tactics, like acting matronly or pretending they didn't understand jokes about rabbits having quiet sex because they have cotton balls. We saw who had the power, and we also saw what happened to those who tried to fight back. In medicine, no one can hear you scream.

"If every state makes up their own rules, why do we even need commissions? Other sports, like baseball and football, they don't have sanctioning bodies, do they?" I asked Dr. Landau. The conference was over for the day, and he had invited a group of us out to a Mexican restaurant for a lesson on tequila. It was one of those indoor–outdoor Vegas places, where the outside was still inside, under a ceiling of fake clouds. Since it was only four thirty in the afternoon, the place was almost empty.

"Commissions and sanctioning bodies are two different things. The commissions are how boxing is even allowed to happen. It's illegal to fight another person with the intent to do harm. It violates criminal law, even if they are consenting adults," he said. "So the commissions are the states' way of getting around the law."

"Did you know that if a professional fighter gets into a street fight, it's considered assault with a deadly weapon?" Dr. Gonzalez added.

"No way!" I said, incredulous.

"Yeah, a fighter has to announce it before he fights,

or he could get in trouble for attempted murder," Dr. Gonzalez said. "Back in the day, fighting and killing in public was normal if you had a good reason. Duels used to be legal, remember?"

"Thankfully, not anymore," said Dr. Rosenberg, an orthopedic surgeon from Westchester.

"Sanctioning bodies are the groups that give out belts and titles and things. And here's where it gets really complicated. There are—get this—*four* sanctioning bodies. There's the World Boxing Council, the World Boxing Association, the World Boxing Organization and the International Boxing Federation," Dr. Landau said, pressing his right forefinger onto the fingers of his left hand as he counted them off.

"Why are there so many?" I asked.

"Because everyone needs to be the king," said Dr. Rosenberg. "It's how they get rich. Each sanctioning body has its own rankings and titles, so every time there is a championship fight, they can advertise and make money on pay-per-view. And now there are—what, fifteen to seventeen weight classes? Every weight class has a world title, and there are *four* titles for each division. It's sad, really. There's no such thing as a real champion of the world."

The tequila arrived on two tasting trays, with three glasses each of translucent liquids of differing hues. Dr. Landau explained the differences between each. "For every tequila, there are three main types. First is the silver." He lifted up two glasses of clear liquor. "This is the agave spirit in its purest form. It is bottled straight from the distillation process, so you can taste its sharpness."

The four of us each took a sip from the first glass. It burned my throat, reminding me of the last night I had forced down tequila.

One summer night, I had downed two shots of Jose Cuervo, before driving up and down the main strip in Minot to advertise a party I was throwing to anyone and everyone in my path. The party, which concluded with a knocked-down chimney and a raid by the cops, was a thank-you present to my mother. I had wanted to punish her for giving me one of the greatest scares of my life.

I was sixteen and had just returned from a week of summer camp sponsored by my high school. When I returned home, I waited in the Hardee's parking lot for my mother to pick me up. But she never came.

My friend's mom, refusing to leave me stranded, drove me home, to the house I had been living in with my family for eight years. Embarrassed, I told her not to worry that no one was home and I was sure they had just run to the store for something. But that was only partially true. When I went into the house, it was completely vacant—of people and furniture. My family had moved without telling me, even though I had spoken to my sister two days before. If it weren't for a forgotten box of utensils, my mother probably wouldn't have even shown up when she did, several hours later. "Well," she had said, shrugging, as if that was all the explanation I deserved.

The payback party was the last time I had tasted tequila, and I had avoided it ever since.

"Can you explain how it works with promoters and managers?" I asked, wanting to learn as much as I could about the business side of things.

"Okay, the promoters are the ones that put on the show. They make money through tickets, broadcast rights, pay-per-view, things like that. Then they have to pay each boxer a certain amount of money, win or lose, based on negotiations. That's where the manager comes in. He is the one that tries to get as much money for his fighter as possible. Then he keeps a fee for himself, which can't be more than a third of the purse," Dr. Landau said, taking more tiny sips as he spoke.

"So why are Tom and Frank the ones delivering the payments?" I asked. Before every fight, they carried around large envelopes of blue safety checks with handwritten amounts.

"That's because, in New York State, the promoter has to bond the total purse with the commission so they can't just run off with the money. That way, the fighters know they're gonna get paid."

He picked up another glass. "The next two—and these aren't the best, just what they had on the menu—are the *reposados*. The word itself, *reposado*, tells you what it is. To repose or rest. The tequila is poured into an oak barrel so it can age, anywhere from two to eleven months. It has a balanced flavor, a mix between the spirit and the wood," Dr. Landau said, moving his hands like he was conducting his own mouth. His love of tradition and precision animated everything he did. Even suturing. He still used a metal syringe with individual glass bottles of lidocaine when he anesthetized cuts.

We tasted the two straw-colored liquids, passing them on to the next imbiber before they even reached our prospective gullets. They didn't sting as much as the first two. Like so many things, they were dulled by time and darkness.

"And finally, the *anejos*. These, my friends, are my favorites. They are basically *reposados* that are allowed to age for a year or longer. And, in my opinion, the longer the better. They use old whiskey and cognac barrels, so the flavor infuses the tequila," Dr. Landau said, lifting one of the glasses so we could peer through it. Backlit by the fabricated dusky light of the casino, the amber liquid looked much darker than the others. He closed his eyes and took the first sip, giving the liquor time to coat his tongue and palate, before swallowing it down slowly.

Touching the glass to my lips, I felt my head spin into a slow vertigo. I remembered how I had impressed my residency interviewer by correctly explaining why alcohol makes us dizzy. Alcohol dilutes the endolymphatic fluid in the semicircular canals of the vestibular organ, making the fluid lighter. Every time we turn our drunk heads, the endolymph sloshes around a bit more, making our brains think we are going much faster than we are. My brain already knew I was moving too fast. The alcohol just gave it an excuse.

★ ★ ★

Two days later, a little wobbly from what had become our ritual of afternoon drinks, I went back to my room to get ready for the awards banquet. I let my hair down and changed into a silver Donna Karan dress, reveling in the possibility of finally meeting one of my boxing idols. At the conference, they had announced that the special guest of the night was Oscar De La Hoya. I almost couldn't breathe.

Walking through the casino, I navigated my way through the maze of slot machines and card tables, using overhead signs for guidance. There were no clocks or hints of natural light, merging day and night into one long dusk. It was like call nights during residency, when the only way I could tell the time of day was by what was on the televisions in patient rooms. I breathed in deeply, taking in the fruit-scented air, the music piping in through the sound system slowly seeping into my awareness.

I hummed the song as I strolled, escalating my steps in time with the beat. The song moved from a quiet conversation, the light tap of a drumstick against a rim, to a river of piano, chords pounding out isolation and betrayal. When the refrain came I felt tears well up. I was in over my head.

I stopped, staring straight into the nothing and everything that lay ahead of me. I had spent so much time, treading water to stay above the abyss, I wondered what would happen if I just stopped and let the ocean take me.

"Everyone...knows I'm in...over my head, over my head..."

The banquet room was much like the one from the Cooney Charity fights. But, instead of a ring, there was a table topped with a short podium at one end of the room. Fifteen round tables were surrounded by eight banquet chairs each and adorned with flower arrangements in the center. Were it not for the still frame of the AAPRP logo buzzing through pixels on the projection screen, I would have thought I was at a wedding reception. There was seating for over a hundred people. Apparently, many more attendees were expected at the party than the conference.

I saw Dr. Gonzalez and Dr. Landau and made a beeline over to where they were standing at the bar.

"I'll have an apple martini," I said, answering the question they hadn't yet asked.

"Wow, don't you clean up nice," Dr. Gonzalez said, struggling to focus inebriated eyes on my neckline. His bronzed face betrayed the fact that he skipped afternoon lectures to lounge by the pool.

"You look lovely, Linda," Dr. Landau said, before turning to the bartender to order my drink. I enjoyed his company for so many reasons, but mainly because he was so respectful. Like many men, the twenty years he had on Dr. Gonzalez had given him a chance to ripen into a man of substance and wit. Unfortunately, it also made him too old and too married to be a prospective partner.

As I took my first sip, I heard a commotion. Excited that De La Hoya was about to make his entrance, I readied myself, straightening my dress and sweeping my hair behind my neck. Surrounded by flashes of cameras and the enthusiasm of a gathering crowd, I could only make out a broad-shouldered man with a navy T-shirt. The mob moved slowly, pausing as it neared us at the bar.

The center of attention was not the man I was expecting. It was Mike Tyson.

"Linda, go! Get over there with him, and I'll take your picture," Dr. Gonzalez said, shoving me into the crowd.

"No," I said, stopping him. "I'm not a groupie." What I really meant was that I wasn't *Tyson's* groupie. I was expecting to meet one of the men who had inspired my love of boxing. Instead, standing less than a yard in front of me was the reason I had stopped watching it.

I found a place at one of the tables, leaving the disappointed Dr. Gonzalez to his own fandom, and took a seat next to Dr. Williams. "I didn't see you at the lectures today," I said. "I didn't know you were coming."

"Ah, I can't sit through those things anymore. I like my time at the tables, if you know what I mean," he said with a dimpled grin.

"Kind of. I'm not much of a gambler, but Dr. Landau showed us how to play craps last night. It was the most entertaining $100 I've ever lost in twenty minutes," I said.

"I see Mike over there. Surprised you're not trying to talk to him like the others. Everyone's always trying to get a piece of him," he said, shaking his head. "You know, I was one of the doctors who defended him during that Holyfield situation. After it happened, the state of Nevada revoked his license. To get it back, he had to go through an independent medical review. They let him choose who he wanted on his panel, and he asked for me. He wanted a brother in his corner."

"So how did it go?" I asked, completely unaware of that aftermath.

"He got his license back to fight in '99 but then lost it again in 2002. For good," he said, in a low voice. "He can't fight for money anymore, but he's doing these exhibition fights. Three rounds, just for show, plain clothes and all that. He just fought Corey Sanders in Ohio; now he's in Vegas training for the next one."

"I want you to introduce me to him," I said, curious. Dr. Williams had defended him, so I figured there must be more to him than the wild animal he had been made out to be. A tortured soul worth saving is hard to resist.

"You know what, let's go over there now. Looks like the crowd has left them alone." He stood and led me to the man who would occupy the rest of my evening.

When they saw each other, they embraced: a man hug that lasted almost a full thirty seconds. What flowed between them was more than just recognition. It was fermented understanding and warmth that grew from standing by someone in their darkest hour.

"Mike, I want to introduce you to one of our doctors. This here is Dr. Dahl," Dr. Williams said, gesturing toward me.

"Oh my gosh, aren't you pretty. You a doctor? Why don't you come over here with me, and let's talk awhile…" Before I could even say hello, he led me away from Dr. Williams to his place at the foremost table to the podium. "Why don't you have a seat here. You so precious." His voice was higher than I had remembered from television, and slow, prolonged by his airy lisp.

The moment we sat, we were surrounded by people taking photographs and otherwise ogling us. He poured water into a glass and set it in front of me. Our conversation had suddenly turned into a public speed date.

"So, tell me about you. What sign is you? You got a boyfriend?" he asked, in one long, unpunctuated string of words. Up close, he was more obtrusive than I had imagined—gap-toothed, thick-faced, round-nosed and tattooed. But he had a sweetness that surprised me.

"I'm a Sagittarius, and no, no boyfriend," I said, with misplaced honesty.

"Yo, Sagittarius! You women *kill* me! I's a Cancer." He shook his head sheepishly, like a teenage boy talking to his crush. Our interaction felt so intimate, the hum of people around us drowned into the background.

"So, where do you live now?" I asked. It was a stupid question, but I didn't know what else to say. I knew very little about his personal life and didn't want to squander the moment.

"I live in Phoenix. Raisin' pigeons." He seemed proud of that, almost beaming. "Homin' pigeons. I just love how they go, and then they come back. It's so peaceful up there on my rooftop…" he continued, talking about his home, his hobbies, his kids.

"Is that Maori?" I asked, almost touching the tattoo on his face.

"You know about that? Sheeeuut! You so precious!" he said.

"I read a lot," I said, referring to one of my favorite books, *The Bone People*. It was about a Maori family and their traditions. The Maori use tattoos, or *ta moko*, to identify tribal associations. Unlike regular tattoos, *ta moko* are considered sacred, carved into the skin by chisels.

"I wish they would just leave us alone so we could talk," he said, referring to the growing crowd around us. If he didn't already feel like a caged animal, I could see how this kind of constant intrusion by voyeurs could drive him there, especially if he couldn't block them out.

"The ceremony is about to start. I should go sit with my friends," I said, standing to leave. "It was nice meeting you." There was no way I could stay there. I didn't know how long I would be able to maintain this conversation, and I wanted to avoid the impending embarrassment of being asked to move by the intended owner of my seat.

"Wait, don't go...or just...come back later. Will you come back?" he asked, more of a plea than a request.

"Of course," I said, surprised at his neediness, returning to my place next to Dr. Williams.

In the time I was gone, the table had filled with Dr. Gonzalez, Dr. Landau, Dr. Rosenberg and their respective wives. They had a lot of questions, each laced with wonder, judgment and jealousy: *What is he like? What was he asking you? Why did you sit there for so long? Weren't you scared? Why were you even talking to him? Don't you know how dangerous he is? Did he hit on you?*

I spoke in vague terms, unsure of the answers myself.

As the banquet wore on, the guests became more inebriated, and the thank-you speeches turned into sermons. But the crowd's attention was still on Mike. He was such an enigma. A tragic hero. Not even violence, jail time or accusations of rape could curtail his popularity. There he was, after everything he had gone through, drinking in gallons of alcohol along with the crowd's adoration. He so badly yearned for love and acceptance and, curiously, he was still open to it. Life hadn't completely hardened him. Somewhere, deep inside, there was still hope. And that hope made me want to forgive him. If he could come out the other side of his life a better person, wasn't that more important than hating him for his past?

By the end of the night, he stood with a group of people, including an eighteen-year-old blonde, for a photograph. Easing in for the shot, he eyed her hungrily. His interest in women included far more than just me.

"It was nice meeting you, Mike," I said, stopping back as promised.

"Wait. Where you goin'? Wanna hang with us?"

"I'm not sure. I have plans," I lied, waving and walking away from him toward the exit. Sitting amid a crowd of people was one thing. Being alone with him was something entirely more dangerous.

"Wait!" he almost yelled, running after me. "Hang with us! Please!"

I looked into his bloodshot eyes. I had stared into that abyss of darkness before. Through Jerome's eyes. They weren't so different, he and Mike. They reacted the same way to fear. But Mike wasn't scared of anything anymore. His worst fears had already been realized, and he was left hanging by any thread. "All right. What did you have in mind?" I relented, watching him visibly exhale in relief.

He wanted to go back to his hotel with his trainer and some friends but, first, we had to make our way through the Luxor to his car. Proceeding toward what we thought was the exit, he entwined his arm in mine, thanking me over and over again for agreeing to come. The five-minute walk was stretched to twenty by the clusters of adoring fans who stopped us every few feet. They wanted a picture of the champ with his presumed wife. Without correcting the misunderstanding, he instead leaned in to my neck and confessed that he wished it was true.

As we approached the Maybach Mercedes awaiting him, I realized that everyone else had disappeared. We were alone. The driver stepped out and opened the door, and I felt pangs of apprehension. I could still walk away. But I wasn't one to walk away from monsters. Not when I was sixteen and my mother had locked me in my bedroom with my 300-pound stepfather to teach me a lesson, collecting bruises like jewelry with each slam against the wall. Or when, three days later, he showed up at my job to take my car and I stood unmoving—outside in the freezing cold—daring him to touch me again.

Mike sniffled as we climbed into the car.

"Are you sick?" I asked, deflecting my anxiety by changing roles. "I'm an ear, nose and throat doctor. I can help with that."

"Nah. I just like to party," he answered, chuckling to himself. He threw his head back and sniffed harder.

I didn't know what partying had to do with having a cold, so I persisted. "I like parties, too, but you don't have to suffer. I could get you some medicine."

He shook his head and smiled, not trying to explain what I didn't understand, then pulled out a small book of photographs. "These here my kids. Five o' them." He named four, stumbling on the last. "He's the little one. Look at them chicken legs—he think he a tough one." He laughed again to himself. "This here's they ma." She was a beautiful, light-skinned black woman who, I remembered reading somewhere, he'd met while he was in prison. She had been a medical resident, and he had been her patient. He must have seen something familiar when he looked into my eyes, too.

We arrived at the hotel, and I was told to wait in the car. Mike went in first, then the driver returned to escort me through the back entrance, up a hidden elevator, to Mike's room. I had never seen anything like it. The palatial living space was encased with floor-to-ceiling glass windows, turning the Las Vegas strip into a living painting. Michael Bublé crooned through the speakers. I relaxed on the couch, watching as Mike rolled the biggest joint I had ever seen and then fell into the chair opposite me.

"So, Doctor, where you from? You so precious," he said before breathing in a huge hit of smoke.

"I'm from the Midwest. My parents are Syrian, but my father's family comes from Chechnya. I'm sure you've never heard of—"

"Chechnya? No shit! I know the president. Me and him is friends." He explained how they had met in the French Riviera when he was there for a "private visit." He told me about the people from the area; how they were warriors and fighters; how he respected them because they were some of the toughest people he had ever met. He knew more about my heritage than I did. "The Russians, they wanted me, too. You know how that goes." I had no idea. "They got a little jealous, so I had to visit them after." He laughed to himself, reliving other memories he didn't want to share, and drew more smoke into his lungs. "You my Chechen queen," he said, squinting his eyes at me. I had always been ashamed of my heritage, but I loved how those words sounded coming out of his mouth.

"Tell me more about you, Mike. Where'd you grow up?" Unlike most people, I didn't know much about his history. In truth, I had never cared before that moment. To me, he was just another angry, violent man who had come into too much fame and money and didn't know how to handle it.

He told me about Cus D'Amato and how he had taken him under his wing and brought him into his home. Cus and his wife had raised him like their own. Except Mike came with a suitcase of rage—rage that could only be harnessed in the ring. When Cus died, so did Mike's sense of security. He was, once again, alone in the world.

He took one last drag from the joint, nearly burning his fingers. "That's enough about me," he said, humming along with the music. He leaned back and coughed, closing his eyes, tapping one foot and then the other. In his reclined position, his oversize belly rose in a mound, cinched in by the waistband of his pants. Rolls of skin gathered around his neck as he settled into the chair. After a few minutes his breathing slowed and, unable to draw air in through his party nose, his mouth dropped open. A tiny snore vibrated across his palate as his chest strained to pull oxygen past his thick tongue. He was in no shape to fight anyone. Not even his own demons.

"Are you tired?" I asked, but he didn't answer. He was already sinking into slow-wave sleep.

I stood and moved closer, studying how the glow of

the light outlined his features. I touched his skin, brushing my fingertips across his tattoo. With closed eyes, I felt its raised edges, following the lines as they wrapped around his left eye—what some cultures believe is our weaker one. This *ta moko* was his shield, a permanent guardian as he looked out onto the world, and the protector against all who looked in. His sleeping face gave away his secrets. His was a tribe of one.

I opened my eyes and got very near to him, so near I could almost breathe in his breath. I kissed his forehead softly. It felt terrifyingly peaceful. Like a prayer.

On the way out of the hotel, I took a different elevator down to the main floor. The doors opened to a large space, occupied by a full-size, empty boxing ring. Posters surrounded the area with pictures of Mike. On the ground, in front of the ring, was a life-size cardboard poster of him, gloved hands on his hips. The reproduction reflected nothing of the man I had just left. Boxing had given him everything and, because he didn't know how to hold onto it, had taken it all away. I wondered what it would try to do to me.

9

Our apocrine glands produce different kinds of sweat depending on how we are feeling. The milky liquid that leaks from our armpits and genitals changes composition and interacts with the bacteria on our skin to create different odors, odors that we inherently understand, even if we don't know why. Because of this, we can literally smell other people's emotions. Sweat can fill the air with an emulsion of anger or drip down limbs and torsos like aqueous anticipation. Disgust smells different from anxiety. Fear is more pungent than trust. What I smelled in this particular dressing room was an admixture of all of those things, with a dash of sulfuric acid from the *micrococcus sedentarius* growing in someone's athletic shoes.

"Which one of you is Bruno?" I asked, looking around the room. No one responded.

I was back at Hammerstein Ballroom, newly anointed with a better notion of my role as a fight doctor—a state-appointed regulator of organized violence. It didn't bother me; in fact, it gave me clarity. I knew I had to protect the fighters from each other, but I had learned that I also had to protect them from themselves, when they hid injuries from me. In the ring, I had the chance to prevent the catastrophic blow to the head before it happened by carefully watching the fights progress. But even that was wishful thinking. Boxers died in the ring. The commission was still dealing with a death that had occurred shortly before I started working the fights.

Through hushed words and fragments of stories, I finally wove together a patchwork of what happened on the *Intrepid*. Docked in the Hudson River off Midtown Manhattan, the World War II–era aircraft carrier had hosted its first and only fight. The boxer who had died was just 26. A last-minute replacement, he went down from a blow to the jaw in the tenth round. After the knockout, he had been taken to the hospital unconscious, but he never woke up. The doctors and commission were involved in a wrongful-death suit and, although they were afraid of the outcome, none of them had quit. His name was Beethavean Scottland. And his spirit had haunted every fight ever since.

Walking through the maze of dressing rooms, I got disoriented. The rooms were so large, they were shared by multiple boxers, and since each had an entourage, they were also filled with men. Men I could barely differentiate. I had one fighter left to check in, and I had to do it quickly because his fight was about to start. "Bruno Castillo? Anyone?"

"Linda, I was looking for you. Can we talk?" It was the

Chairman, walking toward me with a concerned look. Coming out of anyone's mouth, that phrase made me nervous. If someone wanted to talk, why didn't they just talk? Asking about it first created a sense of foreboding.

"I just wanted to let you know, you're doing a great job," he said, in an almost fatherly tone. "And if anyone gives you any trouble, I want you to let me know."

"Why would anyone give me trouble? Everyone is so nice," I said, relieved and a little confused. I didn't know what he meant by *trouble*. No one had belittled or put me down. Unless it was behind my back, I hadn't heard a single sexist comment, and no one had complained about the quality of my work. Yet, for some reason, he felt like he needed to protect me.

"I've been in boxing for over forty years. I know what can happen. I know I don't look it, but I'll be sixty this month," he said. He did look it, but I raised my eyebrows and shook my head in disbelief anyway. The more I got to know him, the more I respected him. He had so much empathy, protecting the boxers like they were his own children. But he was tough, too, with the promoters and managers. I couldn't believe he had only held this position for a few years.

"What day is your birthday?" I asked. Mine was also later that month, nestled in the week of Thanksgiving.

"My birthday is on the 24th," he said.

"Seriously? That's crazy! We have the same birthday! We should celebrate together." I was so overcome with excitement I didn't think about the implications of my words.

The Chairman's expression changed ever so slightly. His eyes softened and creased at the edges. I didn't know why, but I didn't like it. Even if I did, there was no time. I had to get to the last fighter.

"Yo, Linda, Bruno's in the back. You better hurry. He's about to go on," Tom said. He was doing one last circle through the dressing rooms before the show began.

"I can't find him," I said, turning away from the Chairman to look around the room.

"Bruno, yes. *Aquí.*" I heard a voice beckoning me from the far corner. *"Aquí."*

I walked to the source of the voice, past satin jackets and boxing boots, over shards of cut hand wraps and open duffel bags, to one of the most beautiful men I had ever seen.

He was seated forward on a ratty couch, forearms resting on his thighs, a curious look on his face. His eyes locked into mine and wouldn't let go. I sat in a chair next to him and pulled out my blood pressure cuff and stethoscope, trying to ignore the warm glow that burned ever so gently in my chest.

Through darting glances, I pieced together his face. The dorsum of his nose, depressed from repeated blows, was wide and flat, like a baby's. The alar cartilage and columella were all that was left to hold his nostrils up and open, but they weren't doing a very good job, retracting with each inhale. I was taught that we are drawn to beauty because of symmetry, through math and angles and golden triangles. And although his face had none of that, the rest of him seemed unnaturally refined. Lips reflecting light around the margins, philtrum hidden behind their soft fullness. Dimpled chin drawn back into a square jaw. Eyelashes thick like scrub brushes, curled like backward *c*s. Cheeks too abundant to escape a punch, if one ever reached that far. Even folded, his legs looked long enough to take the top of his head above six feet when he stood.

"Who are you?" he asked, stone-faced.

"I'm one of the doctors. I'm here to check you before the fight." I held up my medical equipment as proof. In light of what the Chairman had just said, I hoped he wasn't upset that I was a woman.

He unzipped his warm-up jacket, exposing his brawny chest and more smooth, dark brown skin. His concentrated gaze didn't change as he held out his arm. I wrapped the blood pressure cuff around his sculpted bicep and placed the stethoscope over the inside of his elbow. His veins were thick and corded and floated on the surface of his skin. I inflated the cuff, watching them swell even more until I heard his heartbeat, slow and deep. Releasing the cuff, I watched the dial swing to the left until the thumps faded. Then pressing lightly on his wrist, I felt his pulse. I closed my eyes and counted, long enough to feel the beat escalating through his soft, warm skin. I stopped counting at thirty-five but didn't move my fingers.

"You so pretty," he said. "This place too dirty for you.

Full of smelly old men. Why you here?" He spoke like he valued vowels more than consonants, extending his words like rubber bands.

"I told you. I'm one of the doctors," I said, sticking to my script, praying that it was enough for him.

"No, why you here?" he asked again, emphasizing the last word. I knew exactly what he meant, but it was too complicated to explain. Especially to him. Especially at that moment. "How come I never seen you before?"

I stopped writing his vital signs and looked up to meet his gaze. His eyes had the warmth of genuine consideration, but I knew better than to get into a personal conversation with him. I spent enough time dodging landmines of unwanted attention in my office to let that kind of talk complicate my position here. "I've been around. I've been working with the commission for over a year. We've probably met before," I lied, starting to feel uncomfortable.

"Nah, I'd remember. You beautiful. Where you from?" he asked.

"Your pressure and pulse are perfect, and I've gotta go check out the other fighters. See you after the fight," I said abruptly, cutting him off. I wanted him to stop. Although I couldn't control my internal reaction to him, I could choke it before it penetrated through to the outside. I had found a way of being with these men that was void of sexuality, or so I thought. I realized at that moment that the person most uncomfortable with my gender was me. If I had been born a man, everything would have been so much easier. I wouldn't have felt vulnerable every time I felt attracted or attractive.

"You're an angel," he said as I was leaving. His words felt painful, sweet and hot at the same time. Vulnerability was more terrifying than isolation.

When Bruno ascended into the ring, I hardly recognized him. His black mouthpiece, firmly planted between his teeth, made his face look stern. Every movement of his glistening, oiled body exuded confidence. His eyes were focused on the battle in front of him. He had transformed into something other. The gladiator. The warrior. Raised four feet above the ground, backlit by bright lights, he was terrifyingly majestic.

"Did you know Bruno fought in the Olympics?" Tom asked. He was standing next to me at the edge of the ring, arms crossed, legs spread, head back. He often arranged himself like that when he delivered facts, a position that exaggerated his already long, thin body. "He was on the Puerto Rican team in the late '90s. He was also a Golden Gloves champion."

"He's that good?" I asked, hating that I was growing more impressed.

"Yeah, but he's old already, and he's had some injuries. This is his first fight since his hand surgery. What's it been—seven or eight months, I think? I hope he's still got it in him." Since I wasn't there for his prefight physical, I didn't know his medical history. But I knew what it took to recover from hand surgery. One bad landing could destroy his whole career.

The bell clanged, and the fighters circled the ring. At first, Bruno held back. He studied his opponent, hopping on one foot and moving his neck from side to side like a bobblehead. After what couldn't have been more than fifteen seconds, he moved in to the other fighter and, with one crushing blow, pounded him to the ground. His opponent was out with one punch.

He stood, arms raised in the air, welcoming the cheering crowd. He was victorious and magnificent. The attraction I had fought so hard in the dressing room swept through me like a tidal wave.

He descended the stairs, with a congregation of inspectors, corner men and fans in tow. "Good job," I said.

He barely looked at me, smiling sheepishly as he moved by.

One of the inspectors, a small wiry man with glasses and a stutter, ran through his wake over to me. "H-h-he did it for you!" he said, excitedly.

"What are you talking about?" I asked.

"Before he we-we-we-went into the ri-ri-ring he tol' me, he said, 'I gonna knock him-m-m-m-m out in-n-n-n the first ro-ro-round for the doctah!'"

"He did that for me?" I asked, overcome with so many contradictory emotions I wasn't sure how to feel. Maternal merged with sexual, powerful mutated into vulnerable, attraction morphed into repulsion. But mostly I was speechless.

When it came to male attraction, I was never comfortable. As much as I had yearned for it in high school and college, when it did rear its fickle head, it was never what I expected. In the beginning it felt nice, but that sweetness quickly faded, bringing with it a dark, endless yearning for more. But more of what, it was hard to tell. I thought it was love, that ever-elusive four-letter word that, I learned from my mother and her Harlequin novels, entailed some sort of hunky man making a sweepingly romantic gesture. Wasn't that what had just happened? But that's where the stories usually ended—at the moment of falling in love.

Love. It created a kind of insatiable thirst in me, but the only drink it had offered so far was whiskey. Pungent, sharp, throat-burning sips that left me drunk with desire and even more dehydrated. I had only a headache and heartburn to look forward to the morning after.

Falling. Who would be there to pick me up? The answer was no one. Once the man "got" you, the chase was over. As was the kindness, the attention, and the Feeling Special part. I saw it over and over again in the boys my sister dated, the men my mother married, the patients who were never satisfied by the women they called their wives. In my own husband. I never wanted to be on the taken-for-granted side of love again. Which meant I didn't want to go anywhere near it.

Over time, the men in boxing started acting like the men everywhere else. It took longer than expected, but it happened just the same. Once they saw I wasn't going away, the chivalry faded, replaced by something much more practical: active pursuit. And the more I resisted, the more enticing I became—each man taking a stab at me like I was some sort of carnival attraction. *Come try your hand at the Lady Doctor! One dollar buys three swings!*

At first I didn't mind, letting them play out their charades in front of their friends or in private, because I knew I would never give in.

There was the well-dressed Italian with a thick middle and ambiguous fortune, who pronounced *Italy* with two syllables. He bought me dinner before a fight one night, explaining that he knew how the match would end so it didn't matter if I was late getting back, if I knew what he meant.

There was Cedric Kushner, a promoter, who was once known as Big Ced until he lost two hundred pounds. He noticed me one night at Roseland Ballroom, proclaiming through his slow South African droll that I was "a most handsome woman" that he would very much like to take out. Having made and lost millions, he also had a penchant for the dark side. "You women don't always know what you will like. I've spent a lot of time in houses of ill repute." And even though he moved with the slow gait of a stroke patient, he promised to teach me "a few new moves."

There were countless managers, trainers, friends and fans, egos lubricated by alcohol, who tried to impress me with who they were, who they knew, what they owned, how much money they had. They attached adjectives to my face, eyes, hair, breasts, thighs, ass, as if each comment were a consecration. But, as Frank so honestly put it, they didn't want to "own" me. They were just vultures swooping in to see which part they could steal or borrow for the evening.

As time went on, deflecting the attention became a bigger job than working the fights, but it was a burden I would bear on my own. There was no sense in crying about it or blaming them. I had made the choice to be there. No one was forcing me. I was invading their world. If I wanted to stay, I just needed a better shield. And some weapons.

When the Chairman called my office to invite me to dinner, I had no reason not to accept. It wasn't uncommon for commission members to go out before or after the fights, and none of my colleagues, including him, had made a single inappropriate comment. Although I didn't tell him what the rest of the men were putting me through, I knew that if it ever got too much I could turn to him for help.

We met at an Italian restaurant in Midtown, with the same old-world feel as Gallagher's. Ancient waiters carried bottles of wine and crusty bread, towels draped across their arms. The Chairman was already seated when I arrived but, from the way he was dressed, I worried this night might not go the way I'd expected. Under his sharkskin suit, in lieu of a tie, the first two buttons of his shirt were unbuttoned. On men, open collars usually meant they were open to other things.

"You look beautiful," he said, rising to pull out my chair. "How was your day?" The incongruence of the situation irked me. This was the Chairman, not a potential boyfriend. We were having a work dinner, not a date. I calmed myself with the fiction that he was just being nice. There was no way I could leave, so I smiled politely and decided to make the best of it.

We got our drinks and made small talk until the appetizers came. Once the waiter set down the calamari, all talk of me stopped. We were on to the main event.

He told me he had worked as a matchmaker for four years for one of the promoters. He was the one who arranged the bouts, sizing up the boxers to match their records evenly. That was why he knew all the fighters so well. He was appointed chairman of the commission by the governor almost three years prior and had already made ballsy calls, like suspending a very famous fighter. "He couldn't defend himself in his last fight. I wasn't gonna let him get hurt, not like that," he said, through swallows of bread. "I'm cleaning up the commission. They used to have seventeen fights a year, and now we have over thirty. And no one's gotten hurt."

He continued, telling me how he was a cabbie, then a traveling salesman. At one point, he had enrolled in but never finished law school. He even tried his hand as a ring announcer. "I know everything there is to know about boxing. I want to bring the glory back to

New York." He spoke slowly and carefully, eagerly asking, "What?" every time I mumbled an affirmation. His hearing was a lot worse than he would admit. And it was most obvious in this quiet restaurant, as he struggled to read my lips.

"But all sports, they are like theater. A fight, when you see it live, is like a play. What happens in that ring only happens once. Maybe that's why I write plays. I've written lots of them. I'm a dramatist. I see the drama in things," he said, placing a finger on his chin.

"The play I'm staging now is called *Huckleberry's Garden*. It's about a fireman who lets his captain burn in a fire. He's haunted by the death, and the other guys in his company want revenge." Without warning, his face contorted into a different character than the one he was playing for me. He looked off into the distance and broke into dialogue.

'Huckleberry, you let 'im die! He coulda lived.
I didn't, I didn't know. I tried ta go back...
What kinda man does that?
The place was goin' down! It was him or me...'
He went on like that for a full three minutes.

"And then there's a rookie firefighter, Debbie Mansfield, who's so sexually aggressive she can't control herself. You know women like that." I didn't know any women like that. "She goes after one of the guys, and he has to fight her off."

His voice rose an octave.

'I want you now, right now. I don't care who hears.'
Then back to his deeper voice.

'*I'm a married man. Stop clawing at me, you wretch.*'

He continued, speaking the words in a Brooklyn dialect more exaggerated than his own. The dialogue was so stereotypical, and the subject matter so unbelievable, I could hardly bear to listen. I wished my brain could stop hearing his words.

"What did you think? It's great, isn't it?"

"Oh, yeah. Amazing. You are so, um, multifaceted," I lied. By his enthusiasm, it was clear that no one had told him what they really thought of his work. I wasn't going to be the first.

Our meals came, and he filled himself with another glass of wine and kept talking. "I grew up in Florida until I came back to Brooklyn as a teenager. David Dunkelberger, that's my real name. I changed it when I went into broadcasting. They already had a David Davidson, and I couldn't use Dunkelberger. No way." He shook his head at the audacity of such an ethnically placeable name. "So I created my own." He smiled at his creativity.

Somehow the conversation turned the corner into the dark alley of his childhood. He paused midsentence, suddenly overtaken with emotion. The tears came.

The subject matter had segued into something much too heavy for spaghetti Bolognese. I tried to steer the subject elsewhere, but he returned to his family. I could tell he was no longer aware of me, too trapped in his pain.

He kept talking. There was a girlfriend, who was also a witch. She cast spells to make him stay with her. She also gave him inspirations for his plays.

"I was married once, but we didn't have children," he said. "She was a good woman; it just didn't work out," he said, now four Merlots deep. "Trust me, I've had a lot of girlfriends. I have no trouble with women. But eventually, I lose interest. I'm very picky." He stopped. After nearly two hours of stories and talking and emoting, I prayed that we had finally come to the finale. And we had. Just not the kind I was hoping for. "I knew, the minute I laid eyes on you, that you could be The One."

How had I not seen that coming? I thought I was just being polite, lending an ear, doing what I did when my patients needed to let it all out. We were colleagues, and it wasn't like I could have stopped him with all the waterworks and vomiting up of family secrets. I desperately wished I could go back to Before. To unhear his confessions and unknow his stories.

But unlike the other men, I couldn't just shut him down and walk away. I wanted to be a fight doctor, and he made all the assignments. It was as simple as that. Threatening this relationship meant threatening what I wanted, even though I was starting to question why I wanted it anymore. I let him down gently, but all the wine I'd drunk wasn't doing me any favors.

"David, that's very sweet. I'm so flattered. But…" I grasped at the first thing that came to mind. "We work together. I wouldn't want the other doctors to think you are giving me fight assignments because we are going out." I added important words like *incite* and *undermine* and *integrity*. Official-sounding words to create distance and formality.

"Let them get jealous. We don't have to worry about what other people think," he said. His heart was still melty. It wasn't working.

"Well, what if something went wrong? What if you broke my heart?" I suddenly burst out, remembering how catastrophe happened in romance novels. But my pleading fell on deaf ears. Literally. And only bolstered his already overblown ego.

"Tell you what: let's just keep an open mind and see how it goes." He smiled at me through moist eyes and beckoned the waiter for the check.

In the cab ride home, I berated myself for going down the rabbit hole—again. What was it with me? Was I some sort of homing beacon for broken babies? Or maybe I was so submissive I brought out the worst in men. I also brought out the worst men. I was sick of reacting to what they wanted instead of getting what *I* wanted. I wanted all these men to go to hell and burn in a deep, dark dungeon for their selfishness. I had passed all the same tests, learned the same material and worked just as hard as they had, but it didn't matter. In the end, it was always about them. And all they cared about was getting into my pants.

10

One definition of insanity is doing the same thing over and over again and expecting a different outcome. I had tried to show different parts of myself: the butch, the nerd, the nurturer, the doctor, the Midwesterner. But it didn't matter. I must have been repeating the same patterns because the end result was always the same. No matter what role I tried to play, I was always on the defensive side of my sexuality.

For me, sexuality was a double-edged sword. Too much, and I worried I'd be seen as a slut. Too little, and I might be considered a prude. But I was not a binary being. I had many sides, with dips and curves and U-turns. So many, they often seemed contradictory.

When I was thirteen, my family visited the Middle East for the last time. My father did a sabbatical in Saudi Arabia and took us along for the ride, "to remind you of your real culture," and to show us what hell we'd skirted by being born in the United States. Even though we had heard rumors about the way women were treated "over there," he told us not to worry. He promised that once we got to the town where he would be teaching, he would immediately get us tickets to Syria to see our relatives. He would handle the Middle Eastern culture, since we didn't know how. He would protect us.

As we made our way across the country, strange things happened. The planes got smaller and smaller, the men exchanged pants for long white dresses and the women disappeared, only to be replaced by ghostly figures covered in black from head to toe. By the time we had reached our final destination, a small town outside of Jeddah, I was scared. Even as a newly pubescent teen, I felt the men leering as they quickly shuttled us to an empty dormitory. We would stay in that dorm in near captivity for the next four weeks, while my father secured our exit visas.

It was hard not to feel tricked. Of course he had known we wouldn't be allowed outside without him. He was Muslim and had grown up in this suffocating, punishing culture. Yet, he left us every day at first light, anyway, and returned late into the night or not at all. It was no surprise we went stir-crazy. With no television and only an empty game room and courtyard to keep us occupied, we whiled away the time dancing to pre-recorded tapes of Culture Club and Michael Jackson. We also wrote monotonous tales of woe in our prison diaries.

Today we did nothing.

Today I fought with my sister.

Today I slept for as many hours as my eyes would stay shut.

My father ignored us and our pleas for freedom until two weeks in, when I forced his hand. I'd decided that, if he wouldn't set us free, I would do it myself. The only way a thirteen-year-old girl in a Muslim country could: I would starve myself to death.

Staring at my bony frame, the first and only time anyone called me skinny, I was proud of what my will could do. I knew there was an end date for how long my body could feast on itself in my hunger strike. He couldn't enslave us forever.

When we were finally allowed to walk outside, we floated six feet behind him, ironically liberated by our very own burkas. We were introduced to other women, Syrians, whose husbands worked with my father. They explained that men could not control their desire for women, so we had to completely cover ourselves. Even if we still saw ourselves as children, if we bled between our legs, we were marriageable and, therefore, potential victims. Not even our eyes could show through. If they did, religious zealots would chase us down and beat us with sticks and rocks, which I got to witness firsthand when I accidentally lifted my veil to look at fabrics one evening at a market.

But repression is only one side of a two-sided coin. The other side, the one hidden beneath the flowing garments, was infinitely more confusing. Once indoors, Arabic women removed their dark cloaks to reveal an exaggerated kind of sexuality. Skirt hems were raised to the fullest part of the thigh. Faces were accentuated with dramatic makeup. Bodies were draped in thick ropes of twenty-two-karat gold. Shoes were strappy heels adorned with jewels. One extreme begat another. I was terrified by both.

I was pondering my dilemma with the Chairman and men in general at work one day, when the answer came to me. On its own, and in the form of a woman. She was in her early forties, pretty in an ordinary way, with dark red hair and hazel eyes. Legs crossed in exercise tights, she sat in my exam chair, gesturing with her firm, but not unreasonably toned, arms as she spoke.

"I just keep getting these sinus infections. One every other month. I take really good care of myself, so it doesn't make sense." She looked directly at me when she spoke, one eyebrow raised quizzically, like she was analyzing me.

"How often do you get infections? Do you take antibiotics each time?" I asked about timing, severity, other treatments, what worked, what failed.

Nothing in her medical history seemed to explain her taxed immune system. She was probably around sick people frequently. The worst culprits were small children and the bugs they spread to each other in social gatherings, like playgroups and day care.

"Do you have any kids? Or are you around them, like at work?"

She let out a deep, throaty laugh and shook her head

slowly. "Oh God, no. But sometimes my clients act like children. I won't let them come in if they're sick."

I was intrigued by her response. Clients could mean anything. She could be a personal shopper or photographer. By the way she held herself, back arched, shoulders back, my best guess was a Pilates instructor. I glanced at her intake paperwork. Under employer, it simply said *self*.

"What kind of work do you do?" I asked, mostly out of curiosity.

"I'm kind of a therapist," she said, smiling.

"Really? Like a psychologist?" I could see that. She had an authoritative air about her. And she leaned in at the waist when she answered my questions. Therapists did that.

"Not exactly, although there is quite a bit of psychology involved. For the right person, my work is very therapeutic." She smiled a wicked smile. "I'm a Dom," she said, wrapping her lips around the *m*.

I almost choked. "Wait, *Dom* as in *dominatrix*? Are those even real?" Not only had I never met anyone in her, uh, industry, I hadn't even realized it was an actual thing outside of porn flicks and the internet. I immediately pictured her beating some guy with a whip and tying up his balls. I couldn't help it. Isn't that what Doms did? I had so many questions I could barely connect them into logical strings of words. If I spoke, it would have sounded something like: *How do you find the men are they all men what do you do and how much do they pay you do you*

hurt them and how did you learn how and is it fun? Instead,
I just stared at her with my mouth open.

"I can't really talk about it. You understand. Much like
what you do—client/Dom privilege." She sat back and
crossed her arms in front of her, resolute in her discretion.

"Wait, you can't drop a bomb like that and say you
can't talk about it. What's it like?" I knew she held something vital. Something I needed. I had to get it out of
her, but she was a tough one.

"It's part of the code. I really can't give you details.
There are contracts and rules we must abide by. But what
I can tell you is this. It's not about sex. It's about power.
I am sexual, yes, and I dress provocatively so I can do
my job. That's why it works. When men are attracted,
you can gain control over them. Only a woman can be
a Dom."

"I had never thought about it that way," I said. "I
thought it was about pleasing men. Giving them what
they want."

"Not at all. My clients' only desire is to please me.
They agree to submit to me, so I am in total control."
She tilted her head to one side. "I think you already
understand what I mean."

I did understand. She was describing exactly what I
was looking for—what I was missing in myself. But I
needed to know how she did it. I needed lessons. "Is
there a school or something, where you learn how to *be*
that way?"

She stared at me for a moment, not laughing at my

ridiculous question. "I'm sure there are classes, but they are for beginners. You don't need that. You already have it in you. You're a surgeon, right? Your patients already submit to you every time they lie on the operating table or sit in this exam chair. Then you cut them and hurt them, and they pay you. You're already a Dom. You just need to acknowledge her so she can come out."

I had never thought of it that way. I wasn't a Dom: I was a healer. It took so much abnegation to do this job, I often felt submissive to everyone else's needs. But she had an interesting perspective. If I really wanted to have control over men, I needed to embrace the one part of me I had been trying to avoid the most. I had to own my sexuality like it was a real part of me.

I examined and diagnosed her, then sent her on her way with some recommendations. It turned out she had recently moved into a new dungeon that had a mold problem. The spores had infested her whips and cloth handcuffs. They would need to be dry cleaned to stop making her sick. And I strongly suggested air purifiers.

When we finished the appointment, she thanked me and imparted one last piece of advice. "You need a costume. And a pair of very high, very black boots."

I looked at myself in the mirror. Although I was never happy with what I saw, I didn't exactly hate it anymore. My hair was long, well past my shoulders, but you wouldn't know it. I usually wore it tied into a ponytail or clipped into a homely bun. I resisted a more modern cut because it would require maintenance with things I'd left behind in high school, like hair dryers and mousse. My makeup was also minimal. I limited it to streaks of eyeliner and mascara to enhance the only hair on my body that wasn't thick and long. Although my skin was ruddy and dotted with the occasional bit of acne, I left it naked. Foundation only made it worse, as it did the circles under my eyes that had never quite resolved once the sleepless nights of residency ended.

Although I agreed that the surgeon in me gave me some Dom qualities, I didn't look the part. My patient was right. I needed a costume. The Chairman had said that live fights were like plays. If I saw myself as part of a theatrical experience, I could cast myself in the role of the Dom. The ring could be my stage.

Since I didn't know where to shop for edgier clothes, I walked up and down a few streets near my office to browse. One window display caught my eye. It showcased mannequins laden with plastic jewels and drapey fabric. None of the outfits suited my typical style, but at least they looked stretchy. I decided to give it a try.

"Can I help you?" the sales girl asked, with a pleasant but perplexed look. She was tall and buxom and scarcely older than nineteen. Cheap, capacious jewelry dangled from her ears and neck, clinking against each other like wind chimes. Her lips were traced with liner that was two shades darker than her skin tone and filled in with translucent, shimmery gloss. When I was her age, I was still wearing jeans with real holes in the knees and pumps from Payless.

Since I looked so out of place, I thought about lying that I was looking for something for my niece. But my niece was only twelve. I fought back humiliation and confessed. "I need a suit. A black suit that's fitted, but I also have to be able to move around in it."

She thought a minute and twirled me around, stopping at my behind. "Girrrrrl, you got a booty on you! Baby got back! I've got something for that. It's got a looootta stretch."

In the dressing room I looked in the mirror, twisting from side to side while I formed an opinion. Not bad. But now, the test.

Bracing for disappointment, I squatted low to the ground, fully expecting the pants to burst. To my disbelief, they cooperated, moving with me almost as obligingly as spandex leggings. The side seams, although stretched to their physical limit, held strong. It was kind of a leotard and suit all in one, something I could possibly wear to the gym, if the need arose. And, although the legs dangled from my ankles like mermaid fins, I could easily have them shortened.

As I was basking in my new pant-friends, the salesgirl came by.

"Lookin' good, girl! Wherever you goin', you gonna *rock* that! I got you some tops and jackets to go with those pants. Then you will be da bomb!"

★ ★ ★

"You want to cut your hair off or just change the style?"
Amber the drug rep asked, the next time I saw her. She
had stopped by the office, as she often did, to drop off
drug samples. She had one of those sleek, swarthy New
York haircuts, so I asked her for tips.

"You need to see my hairdresser. He's Israeli, he's hot
and his salon is just a few blocks from here. Tell him I
sent you and he'll give you special treatment." She was so
kind, instantly treating me like a friend instead of a potential sale, now that we were talking about girl things.
As she spoke, I tried to memorize her gestures and movements. She touched her sternum a lot when she spoke.
And the hair toss: I had to remember that, too.

At the salon, the hairdresser was hot, as promised, and
so judgmental he didn't even listen to what I wanted.

"In your office...you are in charge. This...is my office.
Here, I am the boss," he said, combing through strands
of hair to see what he had to work with. "This cut, this
is bad." He snapped his tongue against the roof of his
mouth and lifted his head, the Israeli gesture for *I disap-
prove*. "I will fix. You will also need color."

He painted the roots of my hair with dye and covered
the rest in gloss. Using a razor, he sliced my hair into
wispy layers "to give it height" and just enough bangs
to cover one eye. After the cut, he aggressively blew out
my hair, nearly burning my ear with his metallic round
brush. When he was done, he spun me around to flaunt
the miracle he had accomplished.

I scarcely recognized myself. My hair was shiny and bouncy and nothing I would ever be able to replicate on my own. And the bill was also something I wouldn't be able to repeat. It was over $300 because he insisted on throwing in a hair dryer.

After my parents divorced, when I was finally allowed to adorn my face with pigment, I prided myself on my makeup skills. I studied women's magazines more intensely than my math textbook, researching how to pick the right shade of lipstick and where to dot my cheeks with blush. Stealing into my mother's bathroom, I would emulate the models on the pages, applying thick streaks of eye shadow. My results had more in common with an iridescent peacock than a movie star, but it was the '80s.

But between frozen winters, the poverty of college and the hippie/bohemian fashion it afforded, my skill set was lost.

For my update, I would need professional help. I had seen ads for MAC makeup stores, with bizarrely painted models. RuPaul was their spokesperson. Although it wasn't the look I was going for, it certainly was theatrical. Besides, department-store makeup counters made me nervous, the way the sales ladies peered over displays of lipstick tubes and tried to suffocate me under clouds of perfume. They also judged me harshly for not using moisturizer.

"Hi, sweetie. Do you need any help?" a tiny woman with piercings in her lower lip and eyebrow asked, as soon as I stepped through the door. Her eyes were drawn in with thick, dark liner, carried well past the edges of her eye creases, like a miniature Cleopatra. With half of her head shaved and the other dyed fuchsia, she looked less like a makeup artist and more like a post-apocalyptic anarchist.

"I'd like a different look. Maybe something a little sexier."

"Well, you're not really wearing anything now…you have good cheekbones and such beautiful eyes. I've got some ideas."

She drew her armamentarium from a pouch secured around her waist and patted my face with tan and pink creams, pressing powders on my skin and dusting my eyelids with purples and browns. Her instruments were like a surgical tray, each meticulously crafted for a specific role. Just as it was with the haircut, I had no idea how I was going to replicate this at home. But I was certainly going to try.

When she turned me around for The Reveal, I could hardly believe what I saw. The makeup was stunning in its subtlety, the style so expertly executed that, other than the fact that my eyelids weren't naturally purple, I could barely tell I was wearing makeup at all. Yet, the effect was exactly what I had wanted—sophisticated and polished. And, yes, it was sexy. "You are a magician," I said.

She shrugged and smiled. "Just doing my job." She had done more than her job. Not only had she shown me how good my face could look, she'd also shown me that I could be one thing on the outside without changing who I was on the inside. Just like an actress. Only the whole world was my audience.

11

Patent leather soles clacking on the pavement, I made my way toward the Manhattan Center, barely able to stay upright. After hunting through several stores, I had chosen the shiniest, blackest pair of boots I could find, with heels so tall and narrow they looked like daggers. Walking outside in them, without the luxury of carpeted flooring, was a lesson in New York City sidewalks. With knifelike stabs of pain, they taught the balls of my feet about the density of concrete. Grates and cracks were suddenly everywhere, catching my spikes in their crevices and nearly ripping off the tiny heel caps.

I was ready for the night, but I was also terrified. The shame police who had set up residence in my head told me I was doing something terribly wrong. Doctors weren't supposed to dress this way. But tonight I wasn't myself. Someone else would be wearing my body.

My suit, cloaked by a burgundy lamb's-wool coat, was as tight as my silhouette, clinging to my ribcage with each suffocated breath. I had my hair blown out so straight it moved, solid and liquid, like a particle wave, around my shoulders. I even walked differently, swinging my hips in a slow figure eight, trying to channel my inner Dom with each step. Peering through shimmering shadow and thick press-on lashes, I prayed she would show herself by the time I got to the venue.

When I reached the front door, I stepped up to the security guard and flung my hair back, waiting to meet his gaze.

"Can I help you?" he asked, looking me up and down, interested but unfazed. "Do you have ID?"

"I'm the doctor," I said, jutting my chin forward as I spoke. I opened my black bag and flashed the Athletic Commission badge that had finally come in the mail.

"Wait, you're a *doctor*? I ain't never seen a doctor who looked like you before." Clutching his chest, he leaned back and said, mockingly, "I think there's something wrong with my heart. I need a doctor!"

"Ha ha. I've never heard that one before."

"Be careful in there," he added.

"I will," I said, smiling to myself.

Once inside, I spotted Dr. Gonzalez with Frank and Tom in a prefight huddle near the ring. I tried to calm my impetuous nerves as I approached, setting down my bag and unbuttoning my coat. I stretched back my shoulders to let the coat slide off, but, instead, it got stuck on my upper arms, trapping me like a makeshift straitjacket. Twisting to get free, I inadvertently stretched my low-cut top past my bra, exposing its lace-rimmed décolletage to the three men standing in front of me. They stared in disbelief.

"Hey, guys!" I said, rearranging my top and blocking out what had just happened. "What's my assignment?" I prayed I would be at the corner, so I could go into the ring. The Dom needed a stage.

"Dahl, is that you?" Tom was the first to break the silence. He kept a sober face while trying to camouflage his reaction to my metamorphosis. But his nervous system betrayed him, sending a rush of nerve impulses to his left hand, shaking it like an essential tremor. "Um, Dahl's ringside. Gonzalez you're in the back."

Jackpot.

"Nice outfit, Dahl! You been taking some pointers from the ring girls?" Frank asked, nodding in approval.

"You're looking kind of, uh, different. You look nice, it's just not…" Dr. Gonzalez was noticeably perplexed. And being one of my medical brethren, his discomfort fed into mine, creating a tornado of shame inside me.

Resisting the urge to cover my chest, I instead held my arms awkwardly at my sides and tried desperately to summon my inner Dom. And just like that, she emerged; perfectly formed and fully scripted.

"You're all behaving like you've never seen a female doctor before. Stop acting like idiots, and let's get to work. Fred, start checking out the guys in the back. Frank, stick your tongue back in your mouth, and go find something to do. Tom, give me the paperwork. Anything else I need to know about?" She was a genius, calling all of them by their first names to keep them in their place, then giving them commands, as if they all had to answer to her.

"I, uh, yes, I think. I only got here a little while ago. Let me check," Tom stammered, ruffling through his papers like he was looking for a late homework assignment.

I couldn't believe how easily she'd unhinged them. And how quickly she freed me. With a tiny shift, the Dom had reversed over thirty years of conditioned behavior. But I couldn't get too caught up in the moment. This was just a tiny victory, and her most important audience was fast approaching.

"Hey, guys. You ready for tonight? There're a lotta fights, so let's get through this with minimal injuries," the Chairman said.

"Which corner do I have tonight?" I asked.

His gaze was suddenly different. "Red," he said, then turned to speak to Frank.

I couldn't believe it. The Chairman had never assigned me to the red corner. It was only for the winners.

Beyoncé was going "crazy right now" over the loudspeakers when the headliner entered through the side door of the arena. He danced his way to the ring, hopping and punching the air, opening and closing his lips around the thick blue guard that covered his teeth. The word *CHOC-OLATE* was stretched across the waistband of his white satin shorts, flanked by *KID* on either side. Four men with matching *TEAM CHOCOLATE* jackets followed closely behind. They carried buckets filled with the Dove version of his namesake, showering the adoring crowd with candies. Kid Chocolate smiled and waved, revving up his fans until their cheering made the music inaudible.

I looked out into the crowd: an ocean of men. When I had first started working the fights, they seemed to distribute themselves randomly. Now I saw order: neat clusters of machismo drawn together by a common thread. The Italians clustered together in long black coats, button-up shirts and hair slicked back by hard gel. Teamsters formed a collective, dressed in their least sullied jeans and T-shirts decorated with whimsical sayings like *I only drink beer on days that end in Y.* Then there were the home boys, who stretched do-rags over their short Afros and let big-waisted jeans fall to midthigh. Not to be confused with the gangsters, and those wishing they were, who analyzed the rest of the crowd through bloodshot eyes and unnecessary shades. Other men, hordes of men, filled the spaces in between, hungry for something they weren't allowed in their everyday lives.

I guessed they really just wanted freedom. Comfort and responsibility can create its own kind of oppression. Somehow, the physicality of hunting and catching and killing helped them regain a more visceral sense of who they were. But since that kind of self-expression was no longer allowed in civilized society, they had to settle for being witness to it.

The music changed to reggaeton, the steady under-beat punctuated by alternating rhythms and a handful of boos from the crowd. Kid Chocolate's opponent entered through the same door, bouncing from side to side, head buried under his hoodie like a too-tall, dancing Yoda. Once inside the ring, he pulled back his hood, unveiling a head-shaped display of paisley patterns and letters. From the surface of his left bicep, an elaborate tattoo of a little girl's face smiled at the crowd. He stretched his obliques, ignoring the noise outside his head. After a few minutes, he settled onto the stool at the blue corner, surrounded by his team.

After the announcements and three clangs of the bell, the fight began.

Eyes locking, the two men walked toward the center of the ring. The oily sheen of Kid Chocolate's skin made him look bronzed. He circled his opponent, testing his jab. When he saw an opening, he threw a punch, swiping and missing the moving target of his opponent's head as it jutted backwards.

"Work da jab, work da fuckin' jab! Stop waiting on da jab! Keep it goin'. Right back." A man, straining to contain his enthusiasm, stood behind me, shouting instructions at his fighter. Focused on the action, he leaned in, accidentally bumping my shoulder. My usual reaction would have been to ignore him, but that was not how the Dom worked.

"Excuse me. You need to stand back. This area is for commission only," she said.

"Uh, oh I'm sorry, Miss. I just watchin' my fighter—"

"That's *Doctor*, not *Miss*. You need to stand there." She

pointed a foot away, near an enormous cut man, aptly named Blimp, who was staring at the exchange.

Too shocked to answer, he looked her up and down, hesitating at her chest. She maintained her stance, outwardly unaffected and internally pleased that she had his attention. After a few seconds, he shook his head, remembering where he was, and backed up slowly.

In the ring, Kid Chocolate remained focused, shifting his weight from one foot to the other. Sweat assembled in beads and dripped off bent elbows and knees.

"Underneath, there ya go. Right back. Down da body. Down da body." The same corner man shouted more instructions at his fighter, but with less confidence, glancing over at the Dom apologetically.

Kid Chocolate slowed, grounding his stance. He pulled back his arm and landed one swift punch on his opponent's chin, sending his head back into full extension. Slowly, the other fighter fell backwards, collapsing against the ropes. He staggered, shaking his head, and tried to stand. Worried he would not be able to get back up, I readied myself to climb into the ring, but the Dom held me back.

"Five, six, seven." The referee held his hands within inches of the boxer's face, showing him with fingers how many seconds he had left to recover. When he got to ten, he rubbed the boxer's gloves against his shirt and peered into his pupils to get a read. Satisfied he had enough consciousness to continue, he glanced over at the Dom and nodded. She nodded back.

"Fight!" he said.

Kid Chocolate moved in quickly, chin tucked. His punches were fast and tight, as if his gloves were attached by elastic to his torso. I cringed internally with each blow, feeling the hollowness without the pain, anticipating the one that would finally darken his opponent's soul. Legs already unsteady, he wobbled beneath his weight. He wouldn't last much longer, but the Dom didn't want to stop the fight too early. She knew the value of humiliation, its sour bite and bitter aftertaste. So she waited.

"Uppercut, uppercut! Keep it goin'! Right back." The man behind me yelled in cadence with his fighter's punches, keeping rhythm like a tribal chant.

Kid Chocolate's head moved like his neck was a spring attached to his body. He backed his opponent against the ropes, beating his chest like a slab of meat. Then, seeing his prey relax into the giving-up place, he pulled back his elbow and thrust a mighty punch into his jaw. His opponent's neck twisted toward the ceiling, eyes rolling behind closing eyelids. Legs buckled under deadweight, and he landed flat on the ground. It was a knockout.

Heart pounding, I climbed onto my chair, then stepped over to the table in front of me, wavering in my boots. I steadied myself on the ropes, then climbed between them.

I stood in the ring, suddenly aware of my public unveiling. I felt a hush, possibly real but more likely imagined. I was onstage, and I felt naked. My costume suddenly felt all wrong, too trampy and desperate. The neckline of my top was shamelessly low. My too-tight pants had crawled into uncomfortable crevices. I had been so focused on the knockout, I had forgotten who I was supposed to be. I wanted to cover myself and run.

Looking around the crowd, I took a deep breath. I knew these men, hormones raging through their hearts and groins. They were the real reason I was there, to watch over their gladiators. But I was also there to fight for what was left of me. At that moment, I felt no different than the boxers. I had been knocked down so many times, I had almost forgotten what it felt like to stand back up. But I was standing now. And I wasn't alone. The Dom was with me, anchoring me into my patent leather stilettos. Whatever twisted journey had brought us here, this ring was *her* place at the moment. And she had center stage.

I snapped on my black latex gloves and snapped myself back into character.

The more sauced-up members of the crowd hooted and cheered as the Dom moved in to examine the boxer. I dropped to my knees, thanking the Lycra gods when the pants didn't split. The boxer's nose was bleeding, the blood collecting in a small puddle near his nostrils. Although his eyelids were closed, orbits filled with spongy swelling, the movement in his chest confirmed that he was still breathing. There was no reason to panic. I took my time.

"Are you okay?" I asked, touching his cheek with my

gloved hand. I wanted to see how much perception was left in his body.

Slowly, he pried his eyes open, blinking a few times in the light. "What happened? Is it over?" he asked, more confused than disappointed.

"Well, the fact that we're having this conversation right now means the fight's over, right?" I smiled at him. "Do you know where you are?"

"Yeah, the Manhattan Center. Man, I lost?" His brain was recalibrating nerve impulses into consciousness. The movement must have turned on other reflexes, too, because he sneezed, sending coagulated drops of blood onto my neck, chest and hair. I didn't react.

"Yes, you lost, but you put up a good fight. Most guys don't last that long in the ring with Kid Chocolate. Do you have a headache? Do you think you can get up?" I offered a hand. The blood was hot and wet. I felt nauseated, but the Dom loved it, savoring the blood, a badge of honor.

His corner men were crouched behind me in chaotic discussion. Dr. Gonzalez and Dr. Roy had also made their way into the ring, but stood back with the rest of the crew. They were all awaiting my instructions, even though the boxer wasn't from the red corner.

I beckoned the referee. He helped the boxer to his knees and guided him to a stool. The boxer stared back at me. "I ain't never seen you before. You some kind of manager or somethin'?" he asked.

"No, I'm one of the doctors. When you're ready you can stand up. Take all the time you need."

He did as he was told, using the chair for leverage.

"Now I want you to touch your left glove to your right shoulder—like that, good—and walk heel-to-toe across the ring."

When he got to the opposite corner, he turned and raised his gloves in the air. "I'm good, see?" he said. "So, will I see you at the next fight?"

"Only if you plan on getting knocked out again."

It wasn't until the boxer was nearly out of the ring that Dr. Roy got close enough to speak to me. "There's a fine line between brains and beauty, Dr. Dahl, and you walk that line in very high heels. Nice work. How did you make it up into the ring so fast in those boots, girl?" He was impressed in a way I had never seen before. The usual look of concern hidden behind his glasses was gone, replaced with a kind of reverence.

I looked past his head over to my corner, where a small group of men from the audience was gathering.

"Looks like you got yourself a fan club," Dr. Roy said. "I can't say I blame them. But before you go signing autographs, I've got a fighter in the back who needs your help. He's cut up, and his team requested that you fix him."

The Dom was happy to oblige. Her night was just beginning.

"Let me look at the cuts," I said, taking a seat in the folding chair next to the boxer. The room was otherwise occupied with empty water bottles, dirty towels and two other men milling around in the background. The only light was from incandescent bulbs that framed a mirror on one side of the room.

"'Kay," the boxer said, in a whisper. Lying sideways across an armchair, his head was tilted back. Beads of sweat collected like pearls on his dark skin, the dim light reflecting a glow on the round parts of his face. Eyes closed, he looked like he was in meditation.

"Oooh, you a lucky man, Chop Chop," one of the men said. He looked like he was in his midfifties, from a place with perpetual sun, and he had a paunch that quaked every time he laughed. "You got the pretty doctor!"

I ignored him, took off my jacket and leaned in close to examine the cuts. There were three, two parallel ones over his left brow and one over his right, which were coincidentally symmetrical. Although they were deep enough to expose subcutaneous fat, they were no longer bleeding.

"I'm gonna clean the cuts first, then inject them with lidocaine. A quick pinch, then it'll go numb," I said.

He nodded and kept his eyes closed.

In addition to the essentials, I had stocked my medical bag with enough supplies for a makeshift surgery. On a less-than-sterile surface of paper towels, I laid out my instruments: syringe, alcohol, needle driver, scissors, forceps, nylon suture and gauze pads. Under the muted light of the dressing room, my tools reminded me of what my office patient had said—that I was a natural Dom. In this setting, I saw what she meant.

I wiped the cuts with alcohol, anticipating that he would recoil, but he remained motionless. After drawing lidocaine into a tiny syringe, I made a series of injections into the open edges of the cuts, watching the tissues swell and blanch. After a few seconds, I clamped the curved needle with the needle driver and pricked the edge of the first cut. He didn't wince, so I continued, curling the nylon thread over the wound.

"How old is you?" he asked, his voice barely above a whisper. "Thirty? Thirty-one?" He opened his eyes to get a better look.

"Why do you need to know my age?" I asked.

"You older than that?" He wrinkled his forehead and lifted his head off the chair, disturbing my work area. I held the needle steady, waiting for him to relax and lie back down. Once settled, he continued in a cool voice. "You look young, look good. Mmm." He nodded, studying my face. His mild drawl was southern. "You married?"

"Not anymore, not that it's any business of yours."

Chop Chop leaned in and whispered, "He musta been crazy to leave you." He lingered, his face so close to mine I could feel his breath on my bare chest. I inhaled his attraction, pulling it into me like an electric current.

"I left him," I said.

He smiled and closed his eyes again, enjoying the push and pull.

Tying off the suture, I began working on the next cut, when I noticed that the scruffy man wearing jeans was recording us.

"The guys ain't gonna believe this. I so happy you doin' the cut. We heard about you. The Lady Fight Doctor." He grinned behind his camera.

I ignored him and continued working. "Why did you become a fighter?"

He kept his eyes closed. "The trophies. I wanted the trophies. Started boxin' at ten, kept winning so I kept goin'. I's really good. But you know what I really wanted to be?" His eyes flung open in excitement. "A fashion designer! I looooved makin' the girls' prom dresses in high school. All them other guys said I was gay. But the girls knew I wasn't. Hoooey! Loved all that lace and satin. Mmm. I's gonna do that when I done boxin'." He was smiling broadly now, lost in the moment.

Fashion designer was an unexpected surprise. I wanted to tell him how we shared the same dream, and that someday, I, too, wanted to leave all this behind for the great sewing machine in the sky. But that kind of intimacy was not allowed here.

"Do the guys in your corner know about your *passion*?" I asked.

"Nah. Ah keep it quiet wit dem." His eyes narrowed as if to say *and so should you*. The two men behind us had finished filming and were moving around the room faking jabs.

"There. You're all done. That should keep you together until the next fight."

The scruffy man peered over my shoulder. "Looks great, Chop Chop! Best job I seen."

The boxer sat up and walked over to the mirror.

"What do you think?" I asked.

He studied his reflection, turning his head from side to side to see the stitching from different angles. Pursing his lips together, he nodded and coolly turned, sliding on his shades as he walked out of the dressing room.

As I was leaving, I saw the Chairman out of the corner of my eye. He had avoided me all night, or maybe it was the other way around. I couldn't be sure. I knew I had to confront him and, now that it was about to happen, I was terrified.

"You did really well tonight. I'm proud of you," he said, catching up to me, in his usual fatherly tone. His tie was loosened, his jacket unbuttoned all the way. "I was, uh, wondering if you thought a little more about what I said at dinner."

My usual response would have been to placate him, but that kind of pathetic passive aggression was no longer an option.

"Funny you should mention it. I did think about it, actually. And while I can't blame you for being attracted to me, here's why an affair between us is a bad idea. I am a fight doctor for the commission, and you are the chairman. I want assignments because I am good at what I do, not because I have to sleep with you to get them. If you had any respect for me, or yourself, you would stop trying to get me into bed and start treating me like a professional." I looked directly at him as I spoke. "So, here's how it's going to work moving forward. The only way you will have any contact with me is at the fights. No more personal dinners or phone calls or inappropriate requests. Understood?"

We looked at each other in silence.

"Okay, I get it. I hadn't thought of it that way." He was calmer than I had expected. Perhaps he had heard this kind of rejection before. "You're scared. And you're right. If it doesn't work out, I could break your heart. I don't want you to feel awkward around me."

My blood boiled at his egocentric delusions, even though I was the one who fed them to him in the first place. I wasn't scared or fragile. And, although my heart had been battered, I was strong. I stilled myself, cooling to numbness, and walked out into the cold night air.

12

Once I had had a taste of my inner Dom, it was hard to tuck her away. She was so many things that I wasn't. She didn't care how women judged her. She didn't care what the other doctors said behind her back. Her sexuality was unapologetic. I wanted nothing more than to give her the reins, but I couldn't. The Dom made her own rules, and I lived in a world where I could only survive by following the rules of others.

Medicine is very rigid. From anesthesia checklists to hospital policies, there are no gray areas. But rules aren't limited to scientific facts or surgical landmarks. The whole culture of medicine is inflexible. Doctors communicate in medspeak. We ignore what is right in front of our eyes if it doesn't fit the proscribed differential diagnosis. We condescend when the patient doesn't respond to treatment the way they are "supposed to." Healing that was once an art is now based on evidence and statistics and populations. Somewhere along the way, the group became more important than the individual. Empathy was no longer valuable.

But I was brought up the opposite way, so worried about failing—my patients, my profession, my reputation—that I was willing to do anything and everything to please others. Even if it meant ignoring who I really was. My need for perfection on the outside led to suffocation on the inside. *First do no harm* should have been an oath I also made to myself.

Over the next few months, the Dom's showdown with the Chairman proved fruitful. If he called, it was only to offer fight assignments. When he joined a group of us for drinks after the fights, he bowed out early without trying to corner me with more pleas. I sensed he was biding his time, trying to come up with another strategy but, since I was getting what I wanted, I didn't waste time worrying about it.

In the spring, I was assigned to work the Irish Ropes fights. It was held around St. Patrick's Day every year in the theater at Madison Square Garden. The arena was sizeable—big enough to seat 5,000 beer-infused Celts. That year, a local Irish favorite, John Duddy, was the headliner. He was an energetic fighter whose offensive power made him exciting to watch. It didn't hurt that he was also handsome, all freckles and bright green eyes. His fans included nearly as many women as men.

"You finally get to see Duddy fight," Tom said. He was in his usual tart mood, but something was different. He seemed saltier than usual, but I couldn't put my finger on it.

"I hear he's quite the sensation," I said.

"When he was an amateur, he fought like 130 times and won 100 of those fights. He's only been pro for a few years, but he knocks everyone out in the first couple of rounds. That's why the fans love him."

"Sounds like he was born to fight," I said, feigning punches with my fists. I was trying to be playful, but he wasn't softening.

"Whatever. They are just setting him up with losers so he can build his record. He's an offensive fighter. He can hit, but he can't defend. They won't put him up against anyone good, or it'll ruin his standing." His stubble was a little longer than usual, and by the rainbow of dark colors under his eyes, I could tell he hadn't slept much. I guessed he was having trouble with his on-again, off-again girlfriend. He rarely talked about her, so I suspected this was another off-again period. "You should like this, Dahl. Tonight he's fighting some failure from your neck of the woods."

"Oh, he's from the Bronx?"

"No, this dude, Shelby Pudwill. He's from North Dakota. From a town called Mandan." He said the town's name like it was two words, not two syllables. I shuddered at the mention of it. Just outside of Bismarck, it was even smaller and more insular than Minot.

"What? That's crazy! I didn't even know there were fighters there. Does he even stand a chance?"

"Nah, it's all the same crap. He's just up there feeding the beast like the rest of them."

The fight went as Tom predicted. Shelby went into the ring with Midwestern dignity and a white bandana. But after two knockdowns, at one minute and thirty seconds into the first round, Duddy knocked him out. The loss was quick and decisive and, despite myself, I felt sorry for him.

After the show was over, I found Shelby sitting near the side of the ring. Even though he was a complete stranger, he was more familiar to me than almost everyone I had met in New York. His elongated speech, pale skin, light eyes and lanky limbs incited a visceral response. When I was in grade school, I'd grown so used to looking at pink-skinned blonds I would often fail to recognize my own dark-haired reflection. I felt like an intruder in my own home.

It was unsettling seeing him bloodied, bruised and anemically pale in the fluorescent lighting. He represented people who had caused me so much pain.

"Rough night," I said.

"I'll say. Duddy's no joke. I knew he'd be tough, but I didn't see that coming." He was surprisingly kind and humble, but also completely outside of his element.

"This city's no joke. It's not for the meek."

"Yeah, I can't believe I'm in New York City. Back home, no one could believe I got this fight. They even gave me a big send-off. It will suck to go back and tell 'em I lost. Especially the way it happened." I pictured him at the local truck stop, breaking the bad news to his friends over disco fries and corned beef hash.

"Well, at least you made it here. Not many people can even say that. Do you wanna know something? I grew up in North Dakota, too. In Minot."

"Holy moly, you grew up in Minot?" He pronounced the name of the town the way the city's natives did, with a long *i* and the emphasis on the first syllable.

"Well, I lived there a long time, but I didn't grow up until I left. Thankfully, I got the hell out."

"I can't believe it. I would never think you're from Minot. I thought you were from here, the way you talk and dress and everything." It was the rare person who left North Dakota and, even if they did make it out, a boxing ring in New York City was the last place you would think to find them. He seemed genuinely impressed and suddenly intimidated.

"What is it about the way I look that makes you think I come from New York?" I asked.

"Uh, I dunno. You look, um, uh…"

"Is it my dark hair? My skin tone? I'm wearing clothes that you would never find back home, that's true. Or maybe it's my shape or height? My face?"

Shelby shook his head. "No, it's not that, although you don't look like anyone I've ever seen there. It's more your, uh, attitude. You just seem like a big-city woman."

"Thank you," I said and bid him goodbye.

After he left, a tape that had been running through

my head for far too long slowed to a stop. Its familiar, sad song was of no use to me anymore.

The first time I walked into the main theater at Madison Square Garden, it was empty. Through all my years in New York, I'd never attended an event there. I wasn't a fan of huge concerts and, other than boxing, I had never been to a major sporting competition. I couldn't understand how anyone would enjoy an evening with 18,000 screaming strangers.

I stood at the center of the ring, looking out at the vacant arena, and felt the massive size of the place. There were bleachers and railings as far as I could see. The domed ceiling was concealed by lights and speakers. In the quiet, it was hard to imagine what the place would feel like at capacity. But I would soon find out. It was the day before New York's famous Puerto Rico Day Parade in Manhattan, and this was one of the most anticipated fights of the year.

I had spent enough time with the Dom to gain my own kind of confidence. Less intimidated by her outfits, I learned how to maneuver around more gracefully in heels. I even started re-inhabiting my body when she was there, listening to her thoughts more carefully and mimicking her behavior. I wanted to see how I could be without her tonight.

"I like the suit, Dr. Dahl. Looks like you've taken charge," Dr. Williams said. He was dressed in a silver sharkskin suit, pink tie and a vapor of Issey Miyake cologne. I had come to realize he only attended the important fights. And he always sat ringside at one of the commission tables where he now stood, overseeing everyone else's calls. He needed to navigate from the front row in case things went south. Ultimately, he was responsible. "You working the back tonight?" he asked.

"Yes, I've already checked out all the fighters. Malignaggi's team is here—all twenty-five of them," I exaggerated.

I had heard stories about Paulie Malignaggi, how he was born in Italy and moved to New York with his mother and brother after his parents divorced. As a kid, he was always getting into trouble and, like many fighters, found a place to capitalize on his violence in boxing. Sassy, confident and always surrounded by a gaggle of handlers, he was a pretty boy in the truest sense of the word—with hair styled into spikes or a curly halo. His dark eyes were framed by long lashes and thick, professionally tweezed eyebrows that matched the precision of his hair. At the weigh in the night before, he wore thick gold chains that dangled from his neck, framing bare pecs through a button-up shirt that wasn't buttoned. Despite his years of fighting, his skin was flawless and glowed with the flavor of his homeland.

"Well, Paulie's got a lot of people. And this is a big fight. He's won all 21 of his pro fights, and it's his first time at the Garden. Cotto is the current WBO Junior Welterweight Champion, so he's also fighting for his first world title," Dr. Williams said.

The only thing I knew about Cotto was that he was

from Puerto Rico and always fought in New York the Saturday before his countrymen's parade. When I met him backstage to check his pulse and pressure, he was very serious. I guessed it was because he spoke no English and therefore had no idea what I was saying. Luckily, when the interpreter explained who I was and why I was there, he didn't seem bothered by my being *la doctora*.

"Are you ready for your cameo?" Dr. Williams asked, gesturing around the room.

"What do you mean? Cameo for what?" I asked.

"Tonight's fight is televised. Didn't you say you used to watch *HBO Boxing after Dark*? Well, tonight you may very likely *be* on HBO."

I looked around at what my brain had failed to perceive. Large cameras and *HBO* signs strung the room. *HBO Boxing after Dark*: it brought me back to my apartment in residency, crammed full of unrequited creativity and emptiness. I got flashes of splattered canvases and filthy scrubs. Moldy cheese sandwiches and pizza boxes. It seemed inconceivable that these two realities could exist in the same lifetime.

"The cameras are for the fighters," I said, pragmatically. "I have no interest in being on television." I always laughed at the other doctors when they got excited by it. Even if they were on-screen, front and center, no one ever noticed them. The audience only cared about the fighters.

"You never know," he said, like he had a secret he wasn't going to share.

★ ★ ★

I was standing behind the commission tables across from Dr. Williams when Paulie entered the ring. He was clad in blue satin and white spandex. His black hair, newly bleached at the tips and spiked with gel, was swept off his face by a blue headband. He wore knee-length tights with fringed panels around the waist, embroidered with blue stripes and yellow stars.

I closed my eyes and let my other senses take over. The energy was overwhelming now that the arena was full. I heard fragments of conversations rising over the hum of crowd noise and smelled hoppy notes of beer and sweat. When Cotto was announced, the cheering reached a deafening volume. I felt it vibrate in my chest and abdomen.

After the introductions, the bells clanged, and the fight commenced. The fighters went at each other, easy at first, but hyped with adrenaline. They slowed by the end of the first round, their hormones rebalancing.

I looked behind where I was standing at celebrities I recognized and ones I didn't, interspersed with people who could afford such decadent seats. Unlike the other fans, the A-listers held stoic expressions, presumably so the cameras didn't catch them with an authentic or otherwise ugly emotion. I wondered what made them want to go to the fights in the first place—whether it was genuine interest or just more television exposure.

It was an even match for the first five rounds, each fighter landing blows and combinations that pleased both the crowd and corner men. Between the bells, cut men cooled swollen brows with enswells, while scantily clad ring girls provoked hoots and whistles.

It was the sixth round that changed everything for me. Cotto clocked Malignaggi in the face with a left hook, catching his right cheekbone as he turned his head. It was not so different from his other hooks, but this particular one had just enough force to break the weakest of structures that held up that side of Malignaggi's face: the orbital floor. It was a maxillary blowout fracture. I had seen so many in residency I could diagnose them from twenty feet away. The fracture made his pretty-boy face swell as his sinus filled with blood. If he kept fighting, bits of muscle, fat, nerves and eyeball could fall into the sinus below and cause permanent damage. I needed to tell Dr. Williams.

I looked at him across the ring, but I hesitated. Since I was working the back, I wasn't supposed to interfere with what was going on in the ring. My responsibility was before and after the fights, not during. I could watch the fight, but the corner doctors were in charge. I made my way over to Dr. Roy.

"Paulie has a maxillary sinus fracture," I said, heart pounding so hard I felt my chest move with every beat.

Dr. Roy looked at me like I was speaking in tongues. "What are you talking about?"

"His orbital floor—it's cracked or blown out." I stumbled over my words, unable to make my mouth move fast enough to keep up with my brain. He didn't seem to be getting it. "He could lose his eye," I added. "You have to tell Dr. Williams. He can't keep fighting!"

"Okay, relax. I'll let Dr. Williams know. We'll see what he thinks." He maneuvered his way over to the chief medical officer, and I waited in fear as the two of them spoke into each other's ears, gesturing in the air with cupped hands.

When Dr. Roy returned, I assumed he would have good news and that Dr. Williams would be pleased that I had caught a potentially devastating injury. I was wrong.

"He says Paulie's fine. It's just his mandible."

"What? The mandible is his *jaw*. He's swollen in his cheek, not his jaw. Are you kidding?" Were they blind or just ignoring me?

"I'll check him again after the next round," Dr. Roy said. Between the two of them, he and Dr. Williams had decades of experience working the fights. Was it possible they had never seen this kind of injury? Or maybe they just didn't believe me. Who would listen to a woman dressed like an expensive hooker?

The bell clanged. The fighters were back in the ring.

For the next four rounds, I watched in horror as Cotto pummeled Malignaggi in the face. Blood dripped into Malignaggi's eye like a leaky faucet from an already lacerated left brow. The right side of his face swelled so snugly that his lids sealed together, blocking the vision in that eye as well. He fought back hard until the tenth round, when he became noticeably fatigued. Cotto, still with some reserve left, punched even harder, overpowering him. After twelve rounds, Cotto was declared the winner by unanimous decision. The mostly Puerto Rican crowd went wild.

As soon as the fight was over, before the boxers even left the ring, Dr. Roy rushed over to me. "I need you to look at Paulie. Come with me to his dressing room. Hurry." He seemed suddenly nervous, like he'd finally realized what I had been trying to tell him. Then, it occurred to me—maybe they had believed me after all, but there'd been too much at stake to stop the fight. Now they needed me to clean up the mess.

I followed Dr. Roy in the wake of Paulie's gathering entourage, with cameramen and reporters trailing behind us. We got to the dressing room and shut the door, leaving the rest of the world blind to the real aftermath of the fight.

Somehow the dressing room was already full of wailing grown men. Some yelled phrases of sorrow in Italian, prolonging open vowels to match the extent of their duress. Others spoke with their hands, squeezing fingers to thumbs and raising them up to the heavens, imploring God for forsaking their fighter. As if God cared either way. Paulie was pacing the room, when Dr. Roy took him and me by the elbows and directed us into the bathroom so we could have some privacy. He shut the door, leaving me to assess the damage.

"Oh my God, oh my God… What happened to my face?" Paulie screamed into the mirror, patting doughy cheeks with the fingers of his still-wrapped hands, horrified at the cherubic chipmunk that stared back at him. His skin was mottled like hamburger meat, enveloping his bony understructures like a balloon.

"Let me take a look," I said, grabbing him by the shoulders and turning him to face me. Tears dripped from his eye slits as I placed my thumb and forefinger on his nasal bones and pressed to see if they were broken. They held solidly in place. His nose was dripping blood on my gloves and suit, but it was not coming from a nasal fracture. I pressed on his cheekbones and felt a step-off fracture on the front of his right cheekbone. Just as expected, he had a blowout fracture, but the real damage was much deeper than anything I could assess in a dressing room. His jawbone was the only part of him that was fine.

"I'm going to cover each eye, and I want you to follow my finger. Let me know if you have double vision." I moved my finger to the right and left to see if the muscles that moved his eyes were trapped by fractured bone.

"I can barely see, man. I can't look to the right. Everything is blurry, I see two of everything." He closed his eyes and bent forward, overwhelmed.

As I was about to explain my findings to Dr. Roy, another man burst into the bathroom.

"What's going on here? I need to know. I handle all of Paulie's medical care. I'm his personal physician." He came at me with such authority, my first instinct was to report my medical findings like an intern on rounds. I didn't understand what *personal physician* meant, but I assumed it meant he managed all of Paulie's care.

I went at him with the medspeak. "He has a maxillary blowout fracture on the right, with entrapment of his extraocular muscles, and he has epistaxis, but his nasal dorsum is intact, which means the lamina papyracea is probably broken, too."

Instead of a response, he just stared at me. The same stare Dr. Roy had given me earlier. My inner Dom bristled. "What kind of doctor are you exactly?" I asked.

"Uh, I'm his hand doctor," he said, turning pink.

"You're his *hand* doctor? You have no idea what I'm talking about, do you? I'm getting him to the hospital." I turned to Dr. Roy with more orders. "He needs a CT scan right away. His facial bones will need to be plated sooner rather than later so his orbit doesn't sink into the sinus." Then to Paulie: "Get your things. We're going to the ER."

The moment he walked out of the bathroom, Paulie collapsed onto the floor. The emergency medical technicians ran to him.

"Man down, man down!"

I knelt to the floor, whispering, "Paulie, I know you're fine. Do you need to be on the ground?"

He shook his head and held his face with his hands. He began to cry. "My face, it's ruined. It's ruined. And I lost…"

"You need to pull yourself together," I said. "If you can get up right now, I suggest you do. I know you're upset, but if you can't get it together, they're going to carry you out on a stretcher. How would you feel about that?" He grabbed my arm as I stood up.

"You can't move the patient!" the EMTs yelled. "Lay him back down. Sir, lie down!"

I blocked them from coming near Paulie. "I am the doctor here, and I'm taking responsibility."

"You can't just get him up. We have to follow protocol," one of them said, more used to barking out orders than taking them.

"We have to take him to the ER. He can walk to the ambulance. I'll go with him so he doesn't collapse."

The EMTs, along with everyone else in the room, quieted, watching me lead Paulie down the hall to the ambulance. On our way, we ran into the Chairman.

"Linda, what's happening? Is he okay?" He was anxious in a way I'd never seen.

"I'm taking him to St. Vincent's. He'll go in the ambulance, and I'll take a cab and meet him there."

"I'll ride with you," he said.

When we arrived in the ER, Paulie had already been taken to a room. Even though I didn't have privileges at the hospital, my Dom took charge again, demanding to speak with the ER doctor. I gave him the diagnosis and told him the type of scan to order. I asked to see Paulie, and he led me to the trauma bay.

"I just wanted to make sure you're okay before I leave," I said when I saw him. "I told the ER team what to do. They will take care of you." He was still sobbing, head buried in the chest of a woman I assumed was his girl-friend. Stained with sweat and diluted blood, the once-white spandex tights were sunrise pink. His spiked hair had melted into a sticky mess.

The Chairman followed me out as I was leaving, jogging to catch up to me. "Linda, good work in there. We couldn't have taken care of him without you tonight. He was hurt real bad."

I had so much I wanted to say but felt my actions had spoken clearly enough. I left the hospital, stepping into the warm summer night.

At home, alone in my apartment, I looked into the mirror. The person who stared back was someone I no longer recognized. Blood was smeared on my neck and face, dried into dark maroon segments across my clavicles. Eyeliner was smudged down the side of one eye, and the only remnant of lipstick was an irregular red line, traced around the edge of my upper lip.

You can't get rid of me, the Dom said. *You can't pick and choose when to call on me. Because I am you. I'm the part that wants what you deserve: a part you never knew existed.*

I listened, like I did to the other voices in my head. There was the voice that told me I was broken and not good enough. The voice that kept me glued to the ground in fear. The voice that told me I was fat and ugly. There were so many voices, it was hard to hear my own. But the Dom was louder than all of them.

13

The rumors were circulating.

The chair at the hospital had been replaced by a younger, more driven counterpart, and he was reorganizing the department. At his introductory dinner, I was seated between him and Dr. Marsh, inadvertently playing matchmaker by bringing up common interests. It turned out they had a mutual love of jazz and had since seen a concert or two together.

"During Grand Rounds, I overheard one of the doctors saying he's trying to woo Dr. Marsh back to the hospital," Amber the drug rep had whispered one day.

I didn't believe it. Dr. Marsh would never want to work for an institution. Not after running his own practice. He denied it point-blank when I asked him. "I'm just showing my support for the department," he had said. "And it helps the practice. He offered us extra surgical-block time."

We were so busy with new patients, we could certainly use it.

★ ★ ★

"It's the same stuff. Green snot, you know. I almost brought you some," Mr. Smith said, hanging his suit jacket above his tan leather briefcase by the door. His mucous offering wasn't unusual. Patients often brought in their disgusting excretions, thinking they would help in my diagnosis. But they only made me want to throw up.

"Headache, congestion and cough, too?" I asked. Mr. Smith, along with his wife and children, had been my patients for years. During winter months, at least one of them visited the office every few weeks, passing around illnesses in a game of infectious round robin.

"Yeah, yeah, all those things," he said offhandedly, which was strange. Typically, he enjoyed elaborating on his symptoms. He didn't just have a headache, he had pinpoint pressure just above his left eye. His nose was blocked more on one side than the other, alternating back and forth every few hours and making it hard to sleep. Even though his diagnosis was always the same, he seemed to savor the opportunity to talk about himself. I guessed he rarely had such an attentive listener.

"Is everything else okay?" I asked, regretting the question as soon as it left my lips. Although we had a good doctor–patient relationship, I had learned the hard way that it was best to avoid personal topics with male patients.

He seemed nervous, fidgeting in the seat, shifting his weight from one hip to the other as he contemplated my question.

"I saw you on TV," he said.

"What are you talking about? I wasn't on TV." I thought he had mistaken me for one of those doctors who did spots on the evening news. My practice colleague, Dr. Evans, had done that once. One spring, he was interviewed about rising pollen counts. While B-roll of him walking through the office in his white coat played in the background, the newscaster commented: "City planners choose male trees over females because they don't produce fruit or seeds, which are messy and harder to maintain. But male trees have another job: producing that pesky pollen. With fewer female trees to capture the pollen and filter the air, we are left with more allergens—allergens that get trapped in your nose, making you sneeze and cough." I thought it was hilarious that they were explaining how trees have sex through the air, making our respiratory systems the inadvertent recipients of tree semen.

"It was definitely you. I was watching the fights," he said.

His words filled me with dread. I still hadn't broken the news about my secret life to my bosses, and I wanted to keep it that way. As far as I knew, I had successfully avoided the cameras when they interviewed boxers. I couldn't figure out how I had still ended up on television.

Mr. Smith answered for me. "I saw you on the MSG Network. Does that ring a bell?" he asked, leaning forward in the chair, gaining confidence.

"What's the MSG Network?" I asked, trying to wrap

my head around an entire network dedicated to the toxic food additive that sabotaged my stomach every time I ate Chinese food.

"The Madison Square Garden Network. At the fights. The last fight I saw, the camera was facing you the whole time. At first, I didn't believe it, but it was definitely you. You're a fight doctor," he said, almost accusatorily.

"I didn't realize they televised… I thought it was archival… But I'm never…" I could barely string together a sentence. I wondered how many other people had seen me.

"I *knew* it was you!" he said, brightening. "I'm a huge fight fan! I watch the fights every Friday! How long have you been doing this? Why don't you ever talk about it? This is the coolest—" He recited lists of titles, spouting off winners and weight classes. I half expected him to pull out trading cards.

"I didn't think anyone here—" I gestured with my hands "—would approve. I didn't think boxing was an Upper East Side thing."

"Are you kidding? Everyone watches boxing. I can't always get to the live shows, but I watch the Friday night fights with the guys every week. I can't believe you get to sit ringside and meet all those boxers!"

Softening but still cautious, I shared a little more. "I've been doing it for a couple of years. I get to meet a lot of interesting characters, that's for sure."

"I can't wait to tell my buddies. My doctor—my family's ENT—she's the Fight Doctor! They are gonna be *so* jealous!" He shook his head in disbelief. "Who have you met? Anyone famous?" he asked.

I listed names and fights, their significance affirmed through his responses of "Oh my God!" or "No way!" Through all the conversations we had had about snotty noses and school schedules, I had never seen this side of him. I had always taken him for the Midtown moneyman in the expensive suit. But underneath, he was someone entirely different: someone sweet and funny and rugged. Who would have guessed my dirty little secret would reveal that side of him to me? We all needed shields to live in New York City. We just chose different ones.

As he was leaving, he handed me his card. It listed his company's name, motto—*Excellence in Financial Services*—and his title, *Vice-President*. At the top of the card, the words *boxing fan* were scrawled in his own handwriting.

It wasn't long afterward that the office staff found out about my other life. Before I knew it, boxers were scheduling appointments like regular patients. There was nothing I could do to stop it, and even less I could do to hide them. Compared to my regular demographic, they stood out like sore thumbs.

"Dr. Dahl, you got a cute patient in the next room. He says he already knows you. Some kind of fighter?" The medical assistant smiled. "Is he a boyfriend, maybe?"

I scanned the chart. Indeed, it was a fighter I had met before, but I had no idea why he needed to see me in my office. I did all my suturing in dressing rooms. "He's not a boyfriend," I said, choosing not to elaborate. The less she knew the better.

"Hey, Doc! Great to see you again!" the boxer said when he saw me, jumping up from the exam chair. A full foot taller, he nearly caught my face in his armpit when he tried to embrace me.

"Well, this is a surprise," I said. It was hard to adjust to him out of context, his presence dismantling the walls of my compartmentalized life. "What can I do for you?" I asked.

"I got cut at my last fight, and they sewed me up, see?" He tilted his chin down, pointing to two irregular scars on his brow. "That's why I'm here. My manager doesn't like how they healed. He said you do such a good job, he wanted you to fix 'em." He was more emotive than I remembered, smiling like we were good friends.

I felt both flattered and invaded. I knew my reputation in boxing had grown, but I had assumed it had more to do with my outfits than my work. I had not expected that I'd developed a following among these young men. The prospect left me uncomfortable. The Upper East Side and I had settled into a distant relationship with defined boundaries. The boxers infused my already precarious professional life with an added element of uncertainty.

I donned my headlight and examined his brow and the rest of his face. The frontal projection of his nasal bones were skewed to the right, pulling his dorsum to one side as it made its way diagonally across his face. "You realize your nose was broken, right?" I asked.

"No way!" For someone who had spent the last five years getting punched in the face, his surprise was ironic.

"And it's so blocked, I don't know how you can breathe through it," I continued. His septum, the cartilage and bone that separated his nose into two sides, was internally bent in so many different directions it looked like crumpled tinfoil. It was a wonder any air got through his nose at all.

"It feels normal to me," he said, proving himself wrong by trying to draw air through narrow nasal cavities. After a second or two, he relented, opening his mouth to catch his breath.

Ideally, the nose is supposed to act as a filter, warming and humidifying the air to ease its transition into the lungs. Without the benefit of a functioning nose, our lungs work four times harder to pull oxygen out of the air that comes through our mouths. As good shape as he was already in, his quality of life could be so much better if I fixed the problem. But that wasn't why he was there. "When you're done boxing, we can fix it. Not now. It will just get ruined if you get hit in the nose again," I said, answering his question before he asked it.

"It's a deal. You fix my eye and nose, and I owe you dinner!" he said. I smiled, knowing I would never take him up on the offer.

After explaining the procedure, I went to work on his scars. They were thick, with tiny white circles around the entrance points of the stitches. Hypertrophy was common when silk thread was used, as was often the case when cuts were closed by inexperienced doctors. The same inflammatory reaction that created a thicker bond between the broken pieces of skin also made them ugly. Boxing produced a lot of ugly scars.

Excising the evidence into elliptical shapes, I used a long piece of nylon suture to close the new ones in a continuous running stitch. It was the same stitch I had used for hems in the costume department.

When I finished, I passed him a hand mirror, so he could evaluate his new and improved lines. "I loooook fiiine," he said, drawing out his vowels. "Does that string gotta stay in there?"

"I need to see you back in a week to take it out. For now just put some Neosporin on the cuts. When is your next fight?" I asked, watching as he continued making faces in the mirror, pursing his lips together and sucking in his cheeks.

"Not for another couple of months."

"Good. You'll be all healed up by then," I said, feeling something new and maternal. While I felt obligated to care for everyone who walked through my door, it often felt like just that—an obligation. Taking care of him was different, more personal and meaningful. I had seen him in pain and watched him be brave. And he came in already grateful, already respecting who I was and understanding what I could do for him. Until that moment, I hadn't realized how little joy I got from being a doctor and how much more validating it could be. But I didn't have long to grapple with that realization. The confrontation I had been avoiding most of all was about to confront me.

"What's this I hear about boxers?" Dr. Marsh asked, seated at his desk with his back to me, typing something into his computer. His white coat was neatly pressed and unbuttoned, covering khakis and a plain button-up shirt. Without the benefit of his facial expression, I couldn't tell by his tone whether or not he was angry.

I considered feigning ignorance or making up a story, but I was tired of hiding. Maybe he wouldn't fire me right away. So far, I had been earning my keep in the practice, and he had to give me credit for keeping the boxing thing a secret for so long. He might even give me a second chance or just ask me to quit the fights.

"I've been working with boxers...at fights. It's okay with the malpractice company. I checked, so you don't have to worry..."

He turned to face me. "Slow down, Linda. What do you mean 'working with boxers at fights'? What are you doing to them? Fixing their cuts or something? Like that scene in *Rocky*, where his eye's all swollen?" Switching to another, more rugged voice, he added, "'Cut me, Mick.'"

"No, that was the cut man. I don't do that. I'm a fight doctor," I said, quietly.

"Like that guy, Freddie Pacheco? Didn't he call himself the Fight Doctor?" He was referring to Muhammad Ali's personal doctor, who also worked as a cut man during Ali's fights. His name became synonymous with the sport, although his role bore little resemblance to mine.

"His name is Ferdie, not Freddie. And no, not like him either. I work for the New York State Athletic Commission. Fight doctors are responsible for the medical safety of the boxers. We have to check them before and after the fights to make sure they're okay to continue. We can even stop the fight if we're concerned for their lives," I said, as authoritatively as I could. I wanted him to see that I had a title, and that my role was official.

"That sounds grim. Does it pay well at least?" he asked, which brought up a point I hadn't considered: that working outside my contract with this practice would somehow be a breach.

"Uh, not much. We usually get to the arena around 5:00 p.m. and work until midnight. They pay us $250 for the night."

"So, you make $250 for 7 hours of work? You're a kind soul. I would never do that, especially not for so little. It's hard enough to make it in private practice. How long have you been at it? And why didn't you tell me?"

It was finally my moment of truth. I had to confess everything. "I've been doing it for a little over two years. I didn't think you would approve, so I just kept it a secret." Although I hated how exposed I felt, I was also relieved, like a sinner confessing a hearty sin. At that moment, I felt kind of jealous of Catholics. They could unburden their wrongdoings onto a priest anytime they felt like it. The rest of us had to wait for confrontation.

"Wow! That's really cool! I knew you were doing something outside the office, but I wouldn't have guessed it was something this edgy. Most people wouldn't have been so low-key about it. Actually, it's so gross and violent, I can't think of any other doctor who would want to do it at all. I'm impressed." I couldn't believe it. Not only was he not upset, his words dripped with admiration.

"So, you're not mad?" I asked, still guarded. I was waiting for the other shoe to drop, anticipating a *but*. But that *but* never came.

"Why would I be mad?" he asked. "Did you do anything wrong?"

"No, not that I know of. I just didn't want to embarrass you. I know you've worked hard for these patients, and I didn't want to make you look bad." I needed to air out my assumptions to see if they had any basis in reality—his reality anyway.

"Make me look bad? Linda, I've been watching you for the last couple of years. I've seen how hard you work, and how out of place you are. It's obvious. You came from Minot, North Dakota, for God's sake. I mean, who even lives there?" He chuckled. My residency site director used to say the same thing every time the weatherman announced it as the coldest place in the country. Was I so noticeably awkward? His comment reminded me of what my mother used to say every time I complained that I didn't have any real friends in high school.

"You dress in crazy outfits and act different," she would say. "That's why no one likes you. You stand out, and you're weird. Why can't you just fit in?" The irony was that then, as now, I was expending most of my efforts trying to do just that. But despite my desperate attempts, I seemed destined to be forever out of place.

Dr. Marsh continued. "I watch how you handle yourself. You treat doormen the same as hedge-fund managers. You joke around with the girls in the office like friends. Do you want to know why you are so well liked?" His Buddhism was kicking in, weaving positive affirmations into the conversation. "You don't put yourself above anyone. I was just speaking to the department chair and he agreed. He said we're lucky to have you. You'd have no problem getting a job anywhere you liked. Let me tell you something you probably don't realize: you're a superhero."

I couldn't believe what he was saying. I had no idea he had such a high opinion of me. If he was telling the truth, he saw things in me I would have never seen in myself. I felt embarrassed and self-conscious, but he kept talking.

"You're like Spidey when he first got his Spidey senses. You have superpowers, but you don't know how to use them yet. Remember in the movie, when Spidey couldn't control how he shot out the web? He kept missing buildings when he was learning to fly." He held out his palm and touched his middle finger to its center, simulating Spiderman's hand position. Flicking his wrist forward, he spewed invisible liquid silk around the room to demonstrate. "You're like that—still learning how to use your superpowers. But it will come. Slowly. Just keep practicing."

I let his words sink in, fighting back the urge to cry.

"You need to know this about yourself because I may not always be around to tell you," he said. It was almost too much to take, his understanding and encouragement. I had spent so long feeling like an outsider, I didn't know how to be any other way. But Dr. Marsh, in his endless affirmation, had opened a door for me. All I had to do was walk through.

As a reward for my quick thinking at the Cotto fight, the Chairman assigned me to work the corner for one of my biggest heroes. Wladimir Klitschko was the epitome of brains and brawn. He won gold at the Olympics in 1996, going on to win the WBO Heavyweight Championship from Chris Byrd in 2000. His nickname was Dr. Steelhammer, in reference to his PhD in sports science and his ability to converse in four languages. At six-foot-six, he towered over nearly everyone, save his older brother, Vitali.

Nicknamed Dr. Ironfist, Vitali also had a PhD in sports science. And although he was the only heavyweight champion to have never been knocked down in a fight, he had retired from boxing in 2005, days before his fight with Hasan Rahman because of a training injury. But he wasn't sitting around idle. He had been active in local politics, serving as an adviser to Ukrainian President Yushchenko and running for mayor of

Kiev. Although he lost his first election, he was planning a comeback. In the meantime, he was supporting his brother inside the ring and out.

Waiting to do the intake physical for my fighter, I realized in more ways than one that this fight was bigger than any of the others I had worked. Standing at a cordoned-off section of Madison Square Garden, I watched as the cameramen set up around reporters and folding chairs, readying themselves for the weigh in and staredown. Klitschko's opponent was Sultan Ibragimov, a fighter I had met before when I had interrupted his family's private dinner for a photograph. I didn't realize it at the time, but he was the WBO Heavyweight Champion. Since Klitschko was the current IBF Heavyweight Champion, the winner of the fight would hold both titles simultaneously. This so-called unification of heavyweight titles hadn't happened since 1999, when Lennox Lewis had beaten a double-eared Evander Holyfield.

But shortly afterward, Lewis had retired, relinquishing himself to the sidelines as an announcer.

"I can't believe I get to finally meet Wladimir. I literally can't believe it!" I said to Tom, while we were waiting for the boxers to arrive. The Dom and I had come to an understanding. She was always on call but, if I thought I could handle things myself, she left me to it. She even adjusted to my choice of different outfits, like the dark green button-up shirt and long ponytail I had chosen for the weigh in. The boots were non-negotiable.

"Well, looks like your time has finally come. There

he is," Tom said. Right on cue, in walked an army of gi-
ants. Wladimir led the pack, clad in a black T-shirt and
warm-up pants. I nearly swooned.

"Wladimir, this is Dr. Dahl," Tom said, when Wladimir and his soldiers were seated. "She will be doing
your physical."

I held out my hand to meet his disappointment.

"A woman? I will be checked by a woman?" he said,
visibly offended. Not since Marcos Primera had I been
rejected by a fighter. Whereas before I would've cowered, now I buckled down.

"What, you're afraid of a female doctor? Don't worry,
I don't bite. Let's start with some basic questions. Do you
have any medical problems? Have you had any injuries
or surgeries?"

He leaned back in his chair and rolled his eyes in disgust. Behind him, his brother Vitali paced around, talking
to some of the army in Ukrainian.

"Okay, let's try some more specific questions. Have
you ever had a sexually transmitted disease?" I paused,
wanting to be sure the whole room had heard. But he
wasn't budging. "Do you need me to ask the question
again?"

"No," he said, quietly.

"*No*, you don't need me to repeat it, or *no*, you've
never had a sexually transmitted disease?" I glared at
him, growing more resolute with each passing second.

"*No* to both," he said.

"Good. Do you have any trouble when you pee? Pain

with urination? Weak stream? Does it take a long time to get it all out?" I was completely off book. I had no idea where I was coming up with these questions. Not part of the regular intake physical, they sounded more like the warm-up we were taught to ask before the embarrassing parts of the male physical exam in med school. For lack of willing patients, we were shipped off to the Veterans Affairs hospital to learn how to perform genital and prostate exams on war vets.

Wladimir finally gave me the reaction I was looking for, relenting his pride and answering in one word sentences. When I got to the actual physical exam, there was no more mockery. Even when he nearly knocked me over during the upper-extremity pushback, no one laughed. I remembered a quote, something Vitali had once said: that chess "is similar to boxing. You need to develop a strategy, and you need to think two or three steps ahead about what your opponent is doing. You have to be smart. But what's the difference between chess and boxing? In chess, nobody is an expert, but everybody plays. In boxing, everybody is an expert, but nobody fights." He was right about that. Except he hadn't yet met me when he'd said it.

What happened in the ring was more of a disappointment. Ibragimov was a full four and a half inches shorter and nineteen pounds lighter than Klitschko. His arms were also shorter. He was later blamed for fighting too defensively but, from my vantage, his arm span wasn't

long enough to reach any meaningful parts of his opponent anyway.

Unable to stay focused on all that the fight lacked—
action, competition, brutality, bravery—my mind wandered. Between the boos of the unsatisfied crowd, I
thought of other things I might want to do with my
time: things void of violence and blood and sweat. It
was strange, roaming through that peaceful landscape. I
couldn't imagine a life without fighting.

I thought back to my conversation with Dr. Marsh.
Replaying his words, I sensed an undercurrent. What
if the rumors were true about his negotiating a return
to the hospital? He was spending an awful lot of time
with the chair. There was no way they were just talking about music. He had mentioned that they had even
spoken about me. Now that I reconsidered, maybe his
compliments weren't just compliments. Maybe they were
meant to liberate me from more than my internal prison.
He could be preparing me for something else.

The idea seemed so preposterous I shook my head.
There was no way he would close one of the most successful private practices in Manhattan. No one did that.
It would be a step backwards, and he had no reason to
give up. And now that we had an understanding, I was
starting to feel like I belonged on the Upper East Side. I
needed him. More important, I trusted him.

The fight ended after thirteen tedious rounds.

Klitschko won by unanimous decision. In boxing, there are always winners and losers. But for some, all they had to do to win was show up.

14

"There's a fight coming up next week. I'm having trouble getting someone to cover it because it's in the Bronx. Can you make it up there?" the Chairman asked. He rarely gave me assignments outside Manhattan, so although my initial reaction was a resounding *no*, I felt bad refusing. The two of us had come to a kind of understanding. He still had occasional lapses—a stray comment on my hair or outfits—but for the most part he treated me like one of the guys. And most important, he kept assigning me fights.

"Um, uh, yes, I think I can work that fight. I'll have to look at the train schedule," I said, recalling with dread what traveling was like in the Bronx. Because most of the borough was inaccessible by public transportation, I would have to walk some distance to reach the fight. I thought back to the night my stolen car had been recovered, before the luxury of GPS, when I had had to make my way down Webster Avenue in the dark to pick it up. I had shown up to the parking lot in running shorts and mascara-stained tears, so scared of getting lost or accosted I was delirious. After that, the way I moved through the Bronx changed. I became an aggressive participant, crossing the street when I noticed someone behind me or dramatically turning to look them in the eye so they knew *I* knew they were there. "On second thought, I'll just take a car service," I said, remembering that attackers like easy prey. I couldn't run in heels.

It was late fall, and I was in the car, admiring the last gasps of sunlight peeking over the horizon. I hadn't been to the Bronx since residency, because I'd had no reason to return. The driver took me by Yankee Stadium and onto the Grand Concourse, passing bare-faced brick buildings with eroded whitewash and alternating storefronts of unisex salons and Caridad restaurants.

During the last month of my internship, I had learned a lot about this part of the Bronx. It was June, and the pediatric surgery service was slow. Instead of sitting around waiting for babies in need of emergency hernia repairs, our attending, Dr. Feinberg, had decided to take us on a historical tour of where he had grown up.

He had driven us down a broad, double-wide road, separated by stands of trees. Recalling its heyday, he explained that the Grand Concourse had been originally modeled on the Champs-Élysées in Paris, stretching from 138th Street to Mosholu Parkway. By the mid-1930s, it had become an enclave of upwardly mobile Italian and Jewish immigrants. Some even called it the Park Avenue of the Bronx. The five- and six-story Art Deco apartments, labeled in engraved concrete with names like Majestic Court and the Commodore, had central heating and private bathrooms—coveted luxuries at the time.

"See all these buildings? That block over there is where I grew up," he had said, pointing as he drove. "See that church? Santa Maria something or other? Now, look up at the top. The Star of David—you see that? And the engraving: *Tremont Temple Congregation Gates of Mercy.* All these churches used to be synagogues."

I had been shocked. Beneath the erosion caused by crime and poverty, history was hidden in plain sight.

"And here is where I took my first date," Dr. Feinberg said, pulling up in front of a large, stone building. "This here is the Paradise. It was the largest movie theater in the city at the time and so fancy! We got all dressed up for our big night out—what were we seeing?—I can't remember. Look at those carvings—you can still see the detail. And the clock! That's how I knew when to get my dates home."

Until that tour, I had hated everything about the Bronx. All I had noticed along its streets were used condoms and loose trash. Grocery stores carried food I didn't eat, and bodegas served coffee that tasted like syrup and diabetes. But Dr. Feinberg had shown me that things weren't always what they seemed on the surface. If you knew where to look, you could find beauty beneath the devastation.

My car service pulled to a stop in front of a stone building. I looked up, past carved figures standing at attention, at the huge blue sign. Parts of the words *Loew's Paradise Theatre* glowed in red neon, with sunbeams stretching behind them.

"Dahl, you're late!" Tom said, standing at the front of the theater, the empty stage at chest-level. It was a strange venue for a fight. The audience could only watch from the front, making it more of a bloody stage play than a theater-in-the-round.

"You said 5:30. I—I got here as fast as I could with the traffic—" I stammered.

"Nah, just kidding. The other guys aren't even here yet. You're in back tonight, so you can start hunting down the fighters. There aren't any commission tables, as you can see, so you get to hang with the crowd." Then, snickering to himself, he added, "You get to be with your people again."

"Yes, indeed," I said, wondering how much of me still felt like one of them.

I walked to the back, nearly bumping into Jorge Teron, one of the young fighters I had gotten to know from all the prefight physicals. He was a local favorite and hadn't yet lost in the two and half years he had been fighting professionally. Tall, lanky and usually dressed in ironed jeans, button-up shirts and sweaters, he looked more like a college student than a boxer.

"¡Hola, doctora¡ ¿Cómo estás? You working up here tonight?" he asked, understandably surprised. He had never seen me outside of Manhattan.

"Yeah, the Chairman needed a favor," I said, using the simplest explanation. It was ironic that after working some of the biggest fights in New York, I had ended up right back where I had started. "Why are you here?"

"My friend is fighting. I'm here to support him. We're both from the same hood. We grew up together in the Bronx." His voice was so soft spoken I had to lean in to hear what he was saying.

I remembered after one fight, while I was sewing him up, I had asked him why he had become a fighter. "I needed to be a man for my family," he had said. It was a surprising response for a twenty-year-old, until he explained that when he was fifteen, his mother had been hit by a car. She was crossing a busy street with him and his two younger brothers, and the car had come out of nowhere. Throwing herself in front of her children, she saved their lives but was now a paraplegic and was wheelchair-bound. She could no longer care for her children alone. And, since their father wasn't much help, the burden was left to Jorge's grandmother. And to Jorge.

I knew that street—Broadway, just west of Van Cortlandt Park. I had crossed it many times, walking to the bodega after my runs in the park. It was very dangerous, cars speeding through with no crosswalks or streetlights for hundreds of feet. He and his brothers would have easily been killed had it not been for his mother. I had heard so many sad stories in boxing, and they all had the same thing in common: fighting only became *the* option when there were no other options at all.

An hour later, the crowd began trickling in, bringing with them flashbacks of the Bronx the way I remembered it, filtered through my residency. The exaggerated swaggers of small-time drug dealers. Dr. Haven's huge diamond ring. Blown-out eye sockets. Ear-to-ear lacerations. Dr. Davis's greasy contentment. Pizza and black-and-white cookies with Mosley and De La Hoya. My tiny sense of self.

That was the night you decided to fight. What you had done until then was survive. But that night, you decided you wanted to live.

That night, something had changed inside me. I had wanted to give up, but that fight had made me start fighting for myself. And here I was, back where it had all begun.

The bouts commenced, moving with the same cadence and players, but they felt entirely different. Three-minute rounds and one-minute breaks. Tiny featherweights and huge heavyweights. Judges and referees and inspectors.

Instead of circling the ring between rounds, the Bronx's version of ring girls stayed on the floor with the rest of us. They were so far from the surgically enhanced Manhattan girls that, were it not for their outfits, I wouldn't have guessed they were professionals. One woman, barely eighteen, was dressed in high-top sneakers, a lacy bra and shorts so short there was only enough fabric to cover half of her perfectly round buttocks. Another woman, several years older and much heavier, wore another version of the same outfit—a lesson in ratios, with twice the fabric providing only half the coverage. Together, they taunted men in the crowd, eliciting catcalls and a version of vulgarity that defied interpretation.

"What you lookin' at? What the hell is wrong with you?" the larger one screamed at onlookers as she walked by, her bra straining against the pull of gravity.

"Hey, girl. Ooohweee! Yo ass is fiiiine!" a tiny, stringy man hooted, encouraging a group of men around him to nod and squat to get a better view.

"Yeah? You like this shit? Then you gotta pay, mutha fucka! Git yo ass outta ma way!"

Even though I had never been in her shoes, I felt for her. Without sleep, or safety or personal boundaries during residency, I remembered the rage that came from that kind of vulnerability. A rage that had forced me to choose between playing the victim and taking charge. A rage that had given birth to my Dom. Watching the spectacle in front of me, I remembered the first time I had heard the Dom's voice. It had been tiny at first, echoing my own repressed feelings, but it had become louder through the years, even after I left the Bronx. She had been with me all along, talking in my ear. Daring me to be more than I thought I could be.

After the fight, I joined the other guys from the commission for drinks a few blocks from the theater. Exhausted from the night's revelations, thankful that so many battles were behind me, I collapsed into a seat next to Frank. I wanted nothing but the relief that came from the bottom of an emptied glass. Then the Chairman took the seat next to me.

"Good fights tonight, don't you think? It's not so bad outside the city."

I didn't know how to answer, so I sipped on my drink, hoping he would grow bored with me.

"Can you believe Tyrell, man?" Dr. Rosenberg said. "When he went down in the fourth round, he was totally faking it! I was, like, dude, he didn't even hit you!"

"Yeah, I know," Dr. Gonzalez said. "When he was on the ground, I asked if he was okay. And he was, like, *'I promised them three rounds, and that's what they got.'*" He shook his head and laughed.

I remembered overhearing Tyrell in the back, relaying the rest of the story to his manager as he was changing to leave. "I need to keep my shit intact. I got a wife and three kids. Ain't no one gonna take care of them if something happens to me."

"Do you wanna get out of here? We can share a cab," the Chairman said, nudging me on the shoulder. He never acted this casually, so I thought it was his way of calling a truce.

"Yeah, I need to get home. I have to work tomorrow," I said, draining the last bit of my vodka.

"Why don't you just come home with me? Don't worry—we don't have to have sex. We can just hold each other and cuddle," he said, in full voice, loud enough for the whole table to hear.

I was stunned and disgusted, and there was nothing I could say. Any response on my part, defensive or otherwise, would make it seem like sex and cuddling were things that really happened between us. My colleagues snickered in the background, their lack of surprise belying their true sentiments. I looked at the Chairman, shook my head, stood and walked out the door.

Outside I fumbled with my coat, praying for the very illegal cabs I had avoided when I lived there. Yellow cabs with predictable fares and bulletproof windows never traveled that far north.

"Linda, come on. Why are you so angry?" It was the Chairman again, slightly out of breath from running outside to catch up to me. The cool air formed a vapor around his lips.

"Listen, I'm sorry about some of the things I said to you, about wanting to be with you." He sounded sad and small, like on the night of our dinner. I just wanted to get away from him, but there were no cabs in sight. Bracing for his impending emotional dump, I rolled my eyes and stared down the street, listening as he talked to the back of my head. "I thought you'd see that I'm a good guy, and you'd want to be with me. I'm getting older, and I'm starting to wonder what I will leave behind when I'm gone. I have no children, and most of my family has passed. You can't blame me for wanting to be with you. You're a good person, Linda. I thought together we could have something real."

He was apologizing for the wrong thing, but it was still

an apology. Through our time together, I hadn't considered his perspective or even cared to. All I knew was that he was a man who couldn't take no for an answer, even if that persistence meant invading my personal space. I turned to look at him. In that moment, he seemed like the loneliest person in the world. Even lonelier than me. And he had already wasted so much time, I doubted he would ever be able to give his life meaning.

"Dr. Marsh, I need to tell you what happened last night! I went back to the Bronx!" I said, nearly tripping through his door the next day. Since our little heart-to-heart, he often asked about the fights, wanting to hear gruesome details, but cringing when I delivered them. When I got to his office, I was surprised to find Dr. Marsh's partners seated in chairs across from his desk. They rarely congregated and, when they did, they usually preferred the larger and more comfortable kitchen area. Why they had squeezed into this room was beyond me, but I could tell something was wrong.

"How was it?" Dr. Marsh asked when he saw me, feigning interest. He was clearly focused on something more important.

"What's going on? You guys all look so serious." The door was open, so I didn't think I had walked in on anything secretive, but by the somber looks on their faces, I could tell they were discussing something more pressing than vacation schedules. I paused, instinctively scrolling through the prior week, trying to recall if I had done anything wrong. Nothing stood out.

"We're discussing the practice. The future of the practice, actually." Dr. August spoke first, the most rapacious of the three. He and I had rarely had private discussions and, when we did, it was always about money. When I had first taken the job, he was the one who had negotiated my salary and, after three years, he was also the one who had finally agreed to my small raise. The future of the practice, where Dr. August was concerned, could be anything from wanting to add more patients to my schedule to asking me to buy into their partnership.

"We've been in talks with the hospital, and they want to hire us to be part of the faculty practice. Negotiations have been going on for some time, and we've finally made a decision," Dr. Marsh said, revealing his denials for the lies they had been all along. Apparently, the devil had made a deal that was too good to refuse.

"So, what are you trying to say? They are going to take us over and give us all raises?" I said, trying to make light of the situation. No one laughed.

"We are closing the practice, Linda. The hospital has agreed to hire us as individual faculty," Dr. August said. The most confrontational of the three, I appreciated that he never minced words.

"But why? And what does that mean for me?" I assumed they would have at least negotiated something on my behalf, a comparable salary or benefits package.

After over three years with them, they couldn't possibly abandon me. Dr. Marsh would never let that happen.

"The hospital is willing to meet with you for an interview to see if they have a position that's suitable. You can negotiate directly with them." Dr. August looked straight at me when he spoke, making it clear that it was everyone for themselves. Or, at least, every woman for herself. The three of them had already made deals, and they hadn't advocated for me at all. I would have to start all over again, like I had at the end of residency.

Panic rushed in. "When is this going to happen?" I asked, trying to maintain composure but failing, my voice growing louder and more high-pitched as I spoke.

"The practice will shut down at the beginning of the year," Dr. August said. "I suggest you start making plans right away." It was already mid-October, which meant D day was only ten weeks away.

I turned to look at Dr. Marsh, needing something from him, anything. He was my one ally, the person who had given me hope on the Upper East Side. But he just gazed out the window, refusing to look at me or anyone else.

"Hi, Dad," I said over the phone. "I need your advice." It had been a while since we had spoken. He only wanted to hear news that pleased him, so our conversations usually lasted about five minutes. Real questions and soul searching gave him agita but, desperate for help, I called him anyway.

I could almost see him on the other end of the line,

leaning forward on his elbows at his kitchen counter, thumb on chin, sucking on a Virginia Slim. He only smoked those cigarettes because, as he explained, they were skinnier and therefore "healthy." They also had a mail-away program. He could use the points he collected from his cigarette purchases to order gifts from their catalog. So far, he had earned a jeweled lamp, metal picture frame and duffel bag. One year, he splurged, spending all of his remaining points on a fringed mint-green suede jacket. It was the nicest gift he had ever given me.

"Why don't you just move here to Florida? You can live with me until you find a place and get a job at one of the hospitals," he said, which was his answer every time I wanted to step outside of my comfort zone. It was also never an option. After my parents had gotten divorced, I could barely even visit him. Something about his plastic-covered furniture and empty walls induced within me an unbearable emptiness. So afraid of settling in, he was always three suitcases away from picking up and leaving.

"I was thinking about starting my own practice. I know it sounds crazy, but I've seen other doctors do it. It can be scary at first, but eventually they seem to do okay," I said, hoping he got my hint. Those doctors also had parents or spouses who helped them out. My father had plenty of money socked away for his retirement, which he never planned to use because he was never going to retire. "It is there for you," he would say. "For your future." Well, the future was now, and I needed all the help I could get.

"Linda, you are always acting on your emotions. I know you get mad when I say it because you don't like to hear the truth. You are so sensitive; I have to be careful what I say to you. But I have to be honest. There is so much competition in New York, you will never make it. You should go where they need you, so your success is guaranteed. That's what I teach my students." He had a point. My zip code was so competitive, I had no idea how many of my patients would keep seeing me if I wasn't part of this practice. They would probably just go with someone in the hospital system, like Dr. Patel. Even someone as well respected as Dr. Marsh couldn't make it in private practice. Why did I think I could?

"I get your point, Dad. It's competitive to say the least. But what if I do make it? Could you imagine? You've always said being your own boss is the best, right?" I needed some kind of hope.

"Linda, sweetie, you're just not good at that. I have multimillionaires begging for my advice, and my own children won't even listen. You know nothing about running a business. You need start-up money, probably a couple hundred thousand dollars. Where will you get that?" Not from him apparently. "There are a lot of different types of insurances to protect yourself, like liability and workers' comp. You need a tax ID. You have to hire staff…" He droned on, like he always did when it came to anything business-related. It took all I had to follow the conversation. But I had to admit he was right.

I knew how to do a lot of things, but running my own business was not one of them.

"You need to know your limits, sweetheart," he cooed. "You will never make your own practice work in New York. You shouldn't even try."

15

The next month was a blur. Just when I felt like I finally had a home, the floor had fallen out from underneath me. And finding a job as a doctor was no small feat. Negotiation alone could take months, and then there was credentialing at new hospitals and enrolling in insurance plans. Realistically, the whole process would take at least six months. I only had weeks.

I thought about taking a break to give myself time to consider my options. But even at the risk of jumping into another bad situation, I couldn't afford the luxury of no income. With the exorbitant cost of living in New York, I had very little in savings. And it wasn't like I had anywhere else to go. The only family left in Minnesota belonged to my ex-husband, and my mother's one-bedroom apartment in Fargo was not a realistic option.

After rationalizing Dr. Marsh's abandonment, I agreed to an interview at the hospital. I spent the day meeting with the chairman of the department and faculty members. Dr. Patel, the pretentious physician from that long-ago holiday party was there, too, gloating over yet another private practice biting the dust. After four hours of conversations, tours and discussions, I had to confront the last hurdle before a formal offer. I had to meet with Dr. Sackler.

"So, you are looking for a position here?" he asked, before I had even taken my seat. He was a tall man in his midsixties, with a salt-and-pepper beard.

"I am exploring my options. This is one of them," I lied. I had no other game.

"Well, what do you do, general ENT? I guess we could find something for you. Maybe you could teach the residents. Most of our faculty are fellowship-trained, so you wouldn't really have a place," he said, pulling back his glasses and looking down at my résumé—literally and figuratively.

His condescension reminded me of the time I had interviewed for a job during college in Minneapolis. Sick of working pre-med lab jobs, I wanted to try my hand at something cooler—above my social station. I had applied for a job in a coffee shop with hipsters. The nose-ringed, tattooed interviewer, clad in an edgy thrift-shop ensemble, had taken one look at my waist-high fitted shorts and non-Birkenstock sandals and told me the job was taken. I was not the flavor they were looking for. Which was exactly the message this doctor was relaying to me now.

"Yes, I do general ENT. I see kids and adults. I do a wide range of things," I said. Trying to impress him would have given him more fodder for the attack, so I limited my answers.

"As you know, I am a specialist. I have been part of this practice since I completed my fellowship almost fourteen years ago. And since I also trained at this institution, I am well connected with the administration and the board. You trained in the Bronx, correct? We don't take new hires lightly." He sat back in his chair, elbows resting on the armrests.

"I guess one good thing is that you are a woman," he continued. "We don't have any women in the department, so you could be our first." It sounded more like a threat than a blessing.

He spent the next twenty minutes talking about himself. He had published at least twenty papers, written a couple of books and presented his work internationally, usually at the request of some wealthy entrepreneur. He was so fabulous the president of the hospital himself asked him to perform surgery on his ailing mother. I was surprised that, with all of his accolades, he wasn't able to procure an office larger than his current shoebox. Or that he didn't have a title commensurate with his self-proclaimed success. He seemed like the kind of guy who spent his life staring at himself in the mirror. I couldn't stand one more minute of him. I had endured enough ravings of egomaniacal doctors for a hundred lifetimes. I didn't have the stomach for even one more.

In the end I was offered a salary much lower than the one I had. When I left, I wasn't any closer to knowing where I would end up. But one thing I knew for certain was that it would not be at this hospital.

Searching for other options, I met with a solo practitioner who had built a huge office and operating room suite downtown. He was kind, but his excessive banter would be too much to tolerate on a regular basis. I visited a few smaller practices that wanted to add another partner, but their proposed buy-ins were too high because they wanted more than zero dollars. There was a large consortium of doctors with individual practices and shared overhead, who charged by the hour to use their space. I was used to working nine-hour days, but I didn't have my own patient flow, so the math was just too complicated. One doctor invited me to share his office, but only for a few days a week. Even if I were able to generate enough patients, I wouldn't make enough to support myself without an additional job. A part-time gig picking ear wax out of nursing home patients was not an option. It was an impossible situation no matter how I looked at it.

"I have another fight assignment, Linda," the Chairman said over the phone. It was a Tuesday night, and it had been a couple of weeks since we had last spoken. When he called, I was watching *Grey's Anatomy*, tricked into feeling nostalgic for parts of my residency that had never happened. Unlike Dr. Grey, residents didn't indulge in long conversations over intubated bodies. And no one I knew was having sex in our call rooms.

"I told you, I don't have time for this now. I have more pressing things to deal with—like finding a job." I couldn't believe he had called. I thought I had made it clear that I needed space—from him and boxing.

"Trust me, you'll want this one. Cotto is fighting Mosley." He remained silent for a moment, letting it sink in. "You told me if Mosley or De La Hoya ever fought in New York, you'd want to be there."

That was true. He knew how important that fight was to me, but it had happened nearly nine years before. In my current predicament, it didn't seem to matter as much. "I don't know. Maybe it's best to just leave that part of my life where it is. I need to look forward." There was so little of my past I wanted to remember, even the good parts felt painful in retrospect.

"Just think about it. And, uh, there's something else I need to talk to you about," he said anxiously.

"Oh God, this again? I told you to stop—"

He cut me off. "No, no, it's not that. I got a phone call from someone at the governor's office, and there's a problem. My job's a state appointment and, now that there's a new governor, he has to decide whether or not he wants to keep me as chairman. But I think someone's out to get me. They said they're investigating a sexual harassment claim, and it came from someone in the commission. They said I was accused of harassing you."

I was stunned. Involving state officials was not my style. But with all the rumors flying around about me, any number of people could have done it. Maybe someone had done it to protect me. Or one of the doctors wanted to get back at me for getting so many assignments. Someone from the state probably just wanted him out, and they were trying to use me as an excuse. No matter the reason, I was pleased to see karma exacting its revenge.

"I didn't call it in, if that's what you're thinking. But you have to admit how lucky you are that I was never stupid enough to give in to your come-ons. In the end, I saved you from yourself."

"But I have a good reputation, and I've done good work for the commission. I think they see that—"

"You think they care about that? If they want you out, they came up with an excellent excuse."

"They're going to call you."

"I'm sure they will."

"What will you say?" There was fear in his voice.

"I'm not sure," I said. But it was a lie. Corroborating his behavior would do nothing to serve me. I had handled him, with the Dom's help, and gotten what I wanted—more fights than almost any other doctor. Although for many women telling a state official their story would have a positive impact, it would have done the opposite for me—undermining everything I had earned on my own. The state couldn't erase what I had gone through. If they wanted to get rid of the Chairman, they could come up with any reason. I explained all this to the Chairman over the phone.

There was silence on the other end of the line.

"You're welcome," I said.

"Thank you," he answered, his voice barely above a whisper.

"And, on second thought, I will do the fight," I said, which surprised even me. Boxing was the passionate boyfriend that kept coming back, no matter how many times we tried to break up. Just when I thought it was over, it returned for one more fling.

I walked through the doors of Madison Square Garden, more melancholy than excited. I was still distracted by the dissolution of the practice. Without the push and pull of my Upper East Side–job, the fights felt less pressing. What use was an escape when the very thing I was trying to escape was coming to an end?

"You don't seem yourself tonight. What's going on?" Frank asked. I was surprised he'd noticed. I thought I had successfully camouflaged my inner turmoil behind a new shade of lipstick.

"My job's ending, my bosses are closing the practice and I will have nowhere to work in a couple of months," I confessed. Saying it out loud to him made it even more surreal. It was easier to talk about ring girls than real life.

"Wow, Dr. D, that sucks." He rested his fingers against his temples. "Don't worry. You'll figure it out. You're the kind of person who'll bounce back no matter what. That's why you're here. You're tough," he said, delivering a compliment I didn't feel I deserved. "Well, you better get backstage. Your 'friend' is waiting for you," he continued, smiling like a proud father.

"My friend?" I asked, lost in the moment.

"Sugar Shane Mosley. You need to check him in. He's waiting for you backstage."

My knock on the door was met by a quiet, middle-aged man. He wore a black crew-neck sweater and nodded his freshly shaven head when he saw me, allowing me to pass without asking questions. Inside, the dressing room was quiet, like a monk's chambers. It smelled fresh, with hints of citrus and bleach. The only other person in the room was Shane.

He looked up but stayed seated in his armchair, waiting for me to come to him.

"Hi, I'm Dr. Dahl," I said, outstretching my hand.

In person, he was much smaller than I had imagined, barely taller than me in my boots. His eyes were more blue than gray, with tiny specks of brown near the bottom edges. Round pads of fat and muscle lifted his cheeks to meet his nostrils, which allowed an easy flow of air.

"I need to check your blood pressure and pulse, then I'll be out of here," I said.

"Okay," he said, unzipping his hoodie and extending his arm. In surprising modesty, he covered his bare chest with the free edge of the sweatshirt.

In the silence, with only the hum of ambiguous electrical wiring in the background, I counted out his pulse, slow and steady. Then I inflated the cuff to check his pressure. Listening for the diastolic thump, I was overcome with a sudden yearning. There was so much I wanted to say, but I didn't know where to start or if it would even matter. Of course, it wouldn't matter to him, but I had to get it out for me.

"Everything looks good," I said. I wrapped up the blood-pressure cuff and placed it in my medical bag, hearing the buzz of his jacket zipper closing. It was now or never.

"I usually don't do this, but I have to give you some groupie love," I said.

His expression changed quickly. He leaned away from me with concern.

"No, not like that," I laughed. "I just want you to know how important you are to me. You're the reason I became a fight doctor."

"Really? How's that?"

I told him about my internship and how helpless I had felt. How watching him win as the underdog against De La Hoya had given me the courage to fight my way out of my own situation. How his grace and humility gave him the kind of strength I was still searching for in myself.

"And here you are," he said, a smirk stretching his dimples. "Looks like you made it."

I wanted to cry at that moment and for all the moments boxing had given me. "See you in the ring," I said, my heart swelling with gratitude.

★ ★ ★

"I can't believe he's still fighting. How old is he now?"
I asked Tom. We were standing near the ring before the
main event, and I had just told him about Shane.

"Er, I don't know, in his midthirties, I think," he said.
Then, without warning, "I heard about what happened
with the state."

"What did you hear?"

"It doesn't matter. Don't feel sorry for him. You're
not the only one, you know. He's gone after all kinds
of women. I've heard stories, believe me. He tells that
same crazy shit about his life to anyone who'll listen."
He acted indifferent, as usual, rubbing his facial scruff as
he perused the crowd. He always looked around when
he spoke. I thought it was because he was checking out
the suited men and celebrities seated near the ring, but I
realized, just then, that it was probably his way of main-
taining distance. His emotions were hard to read, but his
actions were always crystal clear.

I shouldn't have been surprised. In my naïveté, I had
singled myself out, even though the Chairman hadn't.
But I didn't want to talk about the Chairman anymore.
I changed the subject. "Isn't there a limit to how long
a boxer can keep going before he hurts something permanently?" I asked. "Some guys keep going forever, but
others get one bad blow to the head, and it's all over."

"Eh—I don't know. It must be genetic or something."
He blended the *eh* and *I* together into a whine. "Look,
there's your friend, Bernard, over there. Talk about fight-

ing a long time. He's—what?—in his forties or something?"

I looked over to where he was gesturing. There, in the front row, sat Bernard Hopkins. And right next to him was none other than Oscar De La Hoya. "Oh. My. God. What is he doing here?" I nearly yelled. I was expecting Shane, but Oscar was a whole different story. The two of them together was almost too much to bear.

"They work together," he said, as if it were obvious.

"What do you mean work together? Like in an office? And how does he know Bernard?" It hadn't occurred to me that fighters going for the same titles could be friends outside the ring. Seeing them root for each other made the whole battle seem like a fraud.

"Dr. Dahl, your simultaneous brilliance and stupidity never cease to amaze me. They work together in Golden Boy Promotions."

"What does that mean?"

"It means that these three guy—Mosley, Hopkins and De La Hoya—are their own promoters. In other words, they've taken the bull by its balls," he said, cupping a proverbial pair in his right hand.

That was genius. Instead of languishing at the mercy of promoters, these guys took control of their own careers by becoming promoters themselves. They negotiated their salaries for each fight *and* made money off ticket sales.

"It's a win–win situation. Win or lose, Mosley's making two million tonight. And that's just for fighting," he continued.

I was impressed. No one could take advantage of them. And, when they were done fighting, unlike Cooney's charity cases, they still had a career. "I have to meet Oscar," I said.

"Then we better head over there now, before the fight starts."

Tom led me past an enormous security guard to where Bernard was seated. I leaned over the barriers that separated the commission seating from the crowd. "Hi, Bernard. Do you remember me?"

"Dr. Dahl, right? Nice to see you." He stood to shake my hand. He was dressed in a dark tailored suit, his tie tucked neatly inside the jacket. I couldn't believe he remembered my name but, because he did, Oscar looked up to see who I was.

"Hi, great to see you, too. It should be a good fight," I said, using empty words to fill the space. I paused, glancing over at Oscar, trying to think of something to say.

"Nice to meet you," De La Hoya said, shaking my hand and saving me from an awkward self-introduction. His hand was warm and strong. Up close, his skin was luminous and, like his aquiline nose, untarnished despite countless beatings. Even without his original music playing in the background, I could see why throngs of women would want to throw themselves at him. He had a magnetism that transcended the television screen. He was a champion.

"We have to go, Linda," Tom said, pulling me away before I could muster up anything meaningful. "The fight's about to start."

"Ladies and gentlemen, welcome to big-time boxing. This is Madison Square Garden, New York City, USA, where tonight, Oscar De La Hoya's Golden Boy Promotions and Bob Aram's Top Rank Boxing are proud to present the Main Event of the evening. Twelve rounds of boxing for the WBA Welterweight Championship of the World... And now, for the thousands in attendance, and the millions watching around the world, ladies and gentlemen..."

The bells clanged, and the fight started, with both fighters going at one another. They pounded gloves into chests, bobbing and weaving, ducking and jabbing. The crowd cheered in approval, cupping their mouths to amplify their screams. Cameras flashed. The chaos and noise blurred into the background. Suddenly it was just me. A moment of stillness. The Dom's voice.

You think you became a fight doctor to get away from your job, but you're wrong, the voice said. *You have it all backward.*

I didn't know how to make sense of that.

You think your life has been hard, and that I came in to save you, but you're wrong about that, too. Why do you think every step of your journey was met with more challenges? The Bronx, the Upper East Side, boxing—even the loss of your job. Just when you get comfortable in one place, you move to

*another with a whole new set of challenges. Why do you think
you made those choices?*

I had made those choices because my career had demanded it. I was just doing what I needed to do. It wasn't
my fault things weren't always what I expected.

I glanced over at De La Hoya, who was cheering, and
I remembered a story I'd once read about him. Despite
his successes, he had never really been accepted by his
community. Born to immigrant parents, he had been
raised in East LA and had grown up between two worlds.
His parents pushed him to fight back against taunting
when he was a kid. By age fifteen, he was already winning titles. When he was seventeen, his mother had died,
but he had kept fighting, winning the gold medal at the
Olympics in her honor two years later, and earning his
nickname, the Golden Boy. This man had believed in
himself. He had created opportunity.

Life is hard, but you always take the harder path, the voice
said. *I came to you in the only way you would understand—
through pain and suffering, beating and blood. You wouldn't
have listened any other way because that was the only language
you knew how to speak. But now, you are me. And I am you.*

And there we were. The we that had become me. Hers
was a tough love, but it was more real than anything I
had ever known.

There is no need to panic. I'm here to help you.

She was right. For the first time in my life, I was free.
If the job hadn't ended, who knows how much longer
I would have stayed? And if I had tried to leave, they

would never have let me out of my contract without a lawsuit. I had spent so much time trying to twist myself into what I wasn't that I had lost track of who I was. I had probably never even known. When had I stopped trusting in the unknown?

I had heard a story once, about a man who went to God and asked him to make him strong. "I want to be strong," he said. "I want to be the strongest I can be."

God said, "Okay, fine. You see that rock over there? Go push it."

The man said, "Okay." So he pushed and pushed. He pushed for days, weeks, months. But the rock wouldn't move. He was patient at first, waking up every morning to try different angles, different positions, different strategies. But it didn't matter. For all his efforts, that rock stayed where it was. Eventually, his frustration got the better of him, and he got angry.

He returned to God. "I'm doing what you said. I'm pushing that rock. I'm trying everything, every day, but it's *not moving!*"

"Just keep pushing," God said. That was all he said.

So the man went back. Some days, he pushed with hope, others with fury. The worst days he pushed with apathy, feeling like he was alone and nothing he did mattered. After years and years of this, he returned to God. If this rock wasn't moving, he wanted to stop trying. He wanted out of this hell he had created for himself.

"Remember what you asked me," God said. "You asked me to make you strong. Look at yourself. Look at your body and your mind. Your muscles are bulging like that guy Atlas I created back in the day. He carried the sky around. Your determination is so unyielding you have the courage to keep coming back to me, whining about wanting to give up. But you haven't. Not yet. You said you want to be strong. I am making you strong. *I will move the rock when you are ready.*"

When it was announced that Cotto was the winner by decision, all the important people rushed the stage. There were inspectors, cut men, managers, trainers, promoters. Oscar was even up there. There they were, Mosley and De La Hoya, hand-in-hand, arms raised to the sky, together right in front of me. Two men I didn't even know, yet had made such an impact on my life. The Golden Boy team had lost the fight but, in my mind, they were still victorious.

I was standing next to the ring as everyone exited. As Oscar passed by, we locked eyes. He smiled broadly and winked. In that moment of mutual recognition, Oscar gave me something more powerful than words of wisdom. He gave me faith. Faith that no matter what, I was a fighter, too.

A week later, I sat in my office at the end of a long workday. Patient charts were strewn across my desk next to my half-finished coffee. I looked out the window at the clothing store across the street and the people rushing home, jackets zipped up against the cold. I only had a handful of weeks left here. It had been my home, even if it had been only a temporary one.

After considering my options for a new job, I had narrowed them down to two, but I was leery. My concern wasn't over success or failure. I was worried I would end up in another situation that would make me unhappy. What was the point of all the hard work if I landed in another place I didn't want to be?

I had moved through my life by making goals. But getting to them had been like driving down a mountain road at night. Looking up, I saw the universe in the night sky and its endless possibilities. Looking straight ahead I saw the twinkling lights of my destination. But what I didn't know—what I couldn't see—was the twisting, winding road it would take to get there.

Near my phone, I noticed a sticky note pressed onto a folder. *Medical accountant*, it read, with a phone number underneath. A friend had given me the name a couple of weeks before. She explained that the first step in setting up my own practice was incorporating and getting a tax ID. "It's simple paperwork," she had said. "You don't even need a lawyer." At the time, the idea had filled me with as much excitement as dread. What had seemed so untenable then, now held a shred of possibility. But all I needed was a shred. If I never tried, I would never know.

For three and a half years, boxing had been my escape from what I didn't want. But I didn't need to escape anymore. And I didn't have to run away to find my power. I had taken this very long journey only to find that my destination had been in me all along. Now, it was time to begin.

I picked up the receiver and dialed.

Epilogue

"There is a patient in room three, Dr. Dahl. He says he knows you from boxing. Did you used to be a boxer?" My medical assistant looked at me quizzically.

"Ha ha, no. I've been many things, but a boxer is not one of them." It had been so long since I had heard from anyone in the boxing world, I had to count the years backwards to be certain.

"Dr. Dahl! Long time! How've you been?" Sitting in my exam chair, cleanly shaven and dressed, as usual, in the same lightweight sweater and button-up shirt, was Frank. He looked almost the same as he had five years ago.

"Give me a hug!" I said, beckoning him to stand, my face landing in his chest. Out of context and years later, it still felt good to see him.

"You're shorter than I remember," he said, pointing at my shoes, which were a little flatter than the stilettos I used to wear in my fight days. My look these days

varied according to my mood. Today, I felt more bohe-
mian than dominatrix.

"This place is amazing. Is it just you here?"

"Yes, it's just me. Do you like it?"

I relayed the story of how my office came to be.
When I had first started the practice, a nearby hospital
took over Dr. Marsh's lease. They had been kind enough
to let me rent part of the space, which had made it easier for my patients to find me when the phone number
changed. After years of searching, I moved to my current location, in Midtown. Tired of the hospital aesthetic
of sterile pastels and institutional prints, I had made my
office warm and inviting—more living room than operating room.

Reality had been more erratic, with fits and starts and
the occasional roadblock. What I didn't tell him was that
I had borrowed hundreds of thousands of dollars to pay
for start-up costs. And because it took so long to enroll
in insurance plans, I had worked for the first six months
without pay. My former bosses had told my patients I
was no longer practicing because I didn't follow them
to the hospital, but the patients eventually found me. I
had hired a manager to set up the business side of the
practice but had let him go a year later when I saw how
he was taking advantage of me. My new practice was
the result of years of planning, saving and building. It
was, as are most valuable things, wrought with drama.
But the end result was worth it.

"It's really nice. I'm proud of you," he said. "When

you left the fights, it was so fast no one knew what had happened to you. We thought, with the Chairman leaving and all, it was something bad." I had heard that the Chairman had been replaced shortly after I left. I didn't know the details, but it seemed more political than anything.

"No, nothing bad happened. I just got caught up in all of this," I said, lifting my palms to the ceiling. "I do miss you guys. That was quite the experience."

"Would you ever come back? A lot of the guys left. Gonzalez and Williams are gone. Dr. Roy works a fight here and there, but there're still no women. It's not the same without you," he lamented. He was still the same man he had always been—loyal, kind and loving. I was lucky to have had him in my corner.

"Thanks, Frank, but that part of my life is over. I have a practice to run. I can't be hanging out all night at the fights," I joked. We continued talking, reminiscing about the old days. There was finally beauty in the past.

As he was leaving, I suddenly remembered that Primera–Stevens fight. Frank had said if things got bad, I should go under the ring. But hiding under that make-shift platform, four feet off the ground, had never really been an option. Maybe that was what differentiated the fighters from everyone else. They didn't avoid the pain. They didn't hide or play it safe. To succeed, they had to be where it all happened—inside the ring, not below it. The beating they took, the beating they gave—that was everything. Because only by facing the pain could they move through it. And for some, for the very lucky ones, on the other side of that pain was life. A life they could define any way they chose.

★ ★ ★ ★ ★

Author's Note

As seen through my eyes, the past has the only perspective it can, and that is mine. I tried to be as close to my truth as possible without causing harm to others. As such, I changed the names of nearly everyone involved, except for the known boxers. I also rearranged the order and timing of some of the fights to fit the narrative of the story. The play, as quoted by the Chairman, was entirely made up by me, but carried the sentiments of his work. The patients I described share traits of several people and do not represent actual people. My parents are a product of their upbringing and environment. Although they were far from perfect, they did the best they could with what life handed them. And, at her request, I left out the existence of my daughter, who was born near the end of my residency.

Also, keep in mind that I started my internship nearly twenty years ago. The Jacobi Hospital I described has long since been demolished and rebuilt. The last fight I worked as a ringside doctor was in 2008, and the commission now functions entirely differently. Most of the people I described in the book have since retired or gone on to other jobs. So this story could only exist when it did, which is in the past.

Acknowledgments

The story of how this book was born is a story unto itself.

Had my daughter not left to visit Yellowstone on a cross-country trip with her father for the summer, I wouldn't have sat at local bars in my vacuum of loneliness and made believe I was a writer. Were it not for Wendy Dale's weekly writing lessons over Skype and endless cheerleading, I would have kept what I wrote between me and the barstool. And when I sent a few chapters to Jane Dystel, instead of encouraging me to find another hobby, she miraculously signed on as my agent. The impossible dream of publishing this book became real when an offer came from editor extraordinaire John Glynn at Hanover Square Press/HarperCollins, who took a huge risk on an unknown neophyte. The entire process happened in less than a year—a year I would have otherwise spent doing what I always did, which was/is doctoring. I wouldn't have known the difference, but now that I do, I couldn't be more grateful.

There are so many more people to thank: Marie Carter

for teaching me Intro to Memoir Writing in the Village a hundred years ago. My staff, Giovanna, Kalyn and Yvonne, for holding the office together while I worked through rewrites. Angela Johnson for her endless encouragement and direction. Diane Moore, for being an all-around awesome younger sister and listening with rapt attention to parts of my life she never knew. David Hess for reading through my entire second draft as I wrote it, offering poignant, sage advice. My daughter, Lucy, for listening to page after agonizing page of my learning process until my writing "no longer sucked." Nansi Friedman, for connecting me with Jane and providing me with endless conversation. Liz Caplan for being a beacon of friendship and light. Charlie Alterman for single-handedly giving the world more joy than it often deserves. My amazing patients who entrust me with their well-being day after day. And the entire theater community for the beauty they put into the world and for giving me a place to finally belong.